His *Grace* Is
SUFFICIENT!

His *Grace* is SUFFICIENT!

A Story of the Search for a Family

JIM DIEHL

Liber Publishing House
www.liberpublishing.com
Hotline: 718 577 1006

Quantity sales. Special discounts are available on quantity purchases by corporations, associations, and others. For details, contact the publisher at above information

CONTENTS

ACKNOWLEDGMENTS

There are so many people I need to thank for their encouragement in writing this short book, but it would be impossible to list all of them. Therefore, I simply want to thank each of them for insisting that I put in writing that which they heard me share from a pulpit or in casual conversation concerning my life growing up as a ward of the state in foster care.

Secondly, I want to thank Annette Allen, my ministry assistant, for her much- appreciated assistance in the editing process. Without her assistance in doing multiple read-throughs and syntax suggestions, this book would fall short of any measure of literary correctness.

Lastly, but certainly not least, I thank the Lord, who has so graciously been with me throughout all the experiences contained in this writing and those not contained.

PREFACE

Upon hearing something of my background and my experiences living in foster homes and an orphanage, many people along the way have encouraged me to share these experiences in a book. My immediate reaction to such encouragement is usually to think, *Why? Who would want to read about me?*

In my mind, writing an autobiography pretty well rates up there with egotism and a self-serving character. However, folks continue to encourage me to write it all down as a testimony— not about me but about what God has done during my short, comparably speaking, lifetime.

So, with that motivation, this is my attempt to set down in print what I have often shared orally in churches and with close friends. It is my singular prayer that, above all else, God will be glorified through this written testimony as I seek to, as accurately as possible, set down some of the major events wherein God has abundantly blessed my life in the good and not-so-good times.

INTRODUCTION

Late Summer, 1951

"Would you mind looking after the boys? I need to go out of town for a while," the young woman asked.

"When do you plan to be back?"

"I'm not sure, but it shouldn't be more than two weeks. I'll let you know."

"Where will you be?" the babysitter asked. "In case I need to get in touch with you—and what about the girls? Who's taking care of them?"

"I'm going out to California with a friend," the woman said. "The two girls will be staying at home with their people."

Two weeks came and went, but the woman did not return. She did send some money to help with expenses for the boys' care, but she never returned. After a while, the money stopped coming.

With that final conversation, two boys—one just short of two years old and the other barely three months old—began a journey which would carry them from one place to another in search of a permanent home; in search of a family.

CHAPTER 1

WHO AM I?

The year is 1956, and I have no idea who I am.

Do *you* know about your infant and toddler years? Do you have photographs to look at that reveal your whole story? Now imagine *not* being able to look back beyond your fifth year of life. Imagine not knowing anything about your parents or family. There are no pictures, no baby books, and no relatives to fill in the gap. It is as though your life began when you were five years old. *Who am I?* The question begins to surface, but there is nothing—nothing—to grab hold of for answers. What would *you* do?

My first memory takes me back to Milton, West Virginia, in 1955. My brother, Steve, and I lived on a small farm in the foster care of the Lewis family. Mr. and Mrs. Lewis had two children of their own—along with at least three other foster children. During those years, I was known as Jimmy Ying. I was four years old and vaguely remember bits and pieces of Easter, summer, and Christmas.

Even in those early days, I remember our family piling into the back of a 1953 black Chevrolet pickup truck and going to church. I can still hear the unique sound of the muffler as we traveled down the dirt road each week. A special memory was the periodic visit of Mrs. Morgan, our "social lady," as she would drop by to take my brother and me to the clinic for shots and checkups. I can still picture her black sedan with the pearl-colored steering wheel and gear shift knob on the column.

Other vivid pictures include cattle grazing on the hillside near our house and the small bridge across the small stream in front of the house. I loved sitting on that bridge, watching the water spiders flit about on the surface and the minnows swimming about. There was a hillside just across the dirt road from the house. Its jutting rocks were a favorite place for cats to hide. It was always a pleasant sight to see and hear the kittens as they emerged from their birth nests among the rocks and indentations.

During the summer, eating watermelon, enjoying popsicles, and anxiously watching for a road grader to scrape the dirt road in front of the house were commonplace. A strange little man with a high-pitched voice pedaled his bicycle past our house daily, calling to us as we would wave and call out to him. All these pictures still bring back warm memories of summer days with the Lewis family.

Equally vivid are the memories of cold winter days. I don't remember playing in the snow, but I do remember snowy days when I would be taken to a loft above the barn where Mrs. Lewis and others would tie tobacco. To briefly explain, the tobacco grown and harvested would be hung in the tobacco barn to cure or dry out. When it was fully cured, it would be readied for the tobacco market by tying several leaves together with another leaf. It seemed that those stairs leading to the upper room were very high, but there were only about twenty steps from bottom to top.

Not intending to be crude about this, I remember being bundled up and taken outdoors to the toilet, which was commonly referred to as the outhouse. Yep, there were no indoor restroom facilities at that time! Well, there was a little white pot with red trim that would be used for light emergencies, but let's not go there. You get the idea, I'm sure. All in all, it was a happy time for all of us.

I only remember sketchy details of the other foster children in the family, but I do remember Jerry, Patty, and Yvonne. I vividly recall Christmas in 1955. I don't really know why—except maybe because it was the year that I got my teddy bear. On Christmas Eve, we were nestled all snug in our beds, anxiously awaiting Christmas morning, knowing that Santa Claus would have made his stop at our house. Jerry and I were in the same bed that Christmas Eve, which probably had something to do with my regular bed being right in the way of getting to the living room where the Christmas tree was set up. I was so excited that I could not get to sleep.

There was no snow that Christmas, and my main concern seemed to be how Santa would get to the house since there was no snow for him to ride his sleigh on. I remember Jerry assuring me that Santa used a helicopter to get around when there was no snow. That worked for me, and the next thing I remember was the sound of a bell clanging at the bottom of the stairs and a hearty "ho, ho, ho" booming up the staircase.

We ran down the narrow staircase to the Christmas tree, which was just a few feet from the stair landing. Presents were everywhere and were quickly doled out to us kids. It was then that I opened the box revealing a brown and yellow teddy bear. It was about two feet tall with plastic eyes and snout and a bright red ribbon tied in a bow around his neck. That bear would prove to be my truest companion for many years to come.

Certainly, there have been many, many Christmases since then, but for whatever reason, that Christmas of 1955 has always stood out as one of the most memorable. You may be wondering how I knew it was 1955, and the answer is quite simple. The following year was to be a monumental year for both Steve and me—a year that would greatly affect our lives even to this very day.

Chapter 2

The Visit

At the beginning of 1956, Steve and I were told that we were going on a visit with our social lady, Mrs. Morgan. On a cold and very snowy January morning, we were bundled up and sent off with Mrs. Morgan for *the visit*. As we came closer to the end of Saunders Creek Road, Mrs. Morgan stopped the car and explained that we were going to visit some very nice people and asked if we would like to stay with these people or just visit. Being the more extroverted one, I immediately responded that I wanted to stay. Steve, sitting quietly in the back seat, hesitantly said, "Just visit."

The snow continued to fall that morning as we pulled into a long driveway that led up to a two-story brick house with snowcapped shrubs along the walkway. As we climbed out of the car and up the front porch steps, we were greeted by a nice lady who invited us to come in and get warm. Other than being introduced to Mrs. DeJarnett, I don't recall what the initial conversation was, but I do recall that we were quickly given a tour of the house.

As we came to the top of the stairs, there was a bedroom to the left and a larger room straight ahead. As we entered that large room, I noticed a section to the right. It was kind of an L-shaped room with a twin bed in each main area. The bed that I was to sleep in was next to the window overlooking the front porch; Steve's bed faced the side of the house above the driveway.

In Steve's section, a small gas stove seemed to adequately warm the entire room. The light switches in the rooms upstairs (and down) were push button. These interested me—along with the stub of a painted galvanized pipe that hung about twelve inches below the ceiling and protruded from the wall six or seven inches. We hung out clothes on the pipe.

I don't really recall how long Mrs. Morgan stayed at the house with us. The next thing I remember was eating an egg on toast sandwich at the kitchen table. The egg managed to slip through the bottom of the sandwich and onto my lap. This didn't seem to bother Mrs. DeJarnett, and she immediately assured me that it was okay. To wash down the sandwich, we were given some hot chocolate. During lunch, the conversation concerned how long we would be staying with the DeJarnett family. Steve, again, commented that we would just be visiting, but I insisted that we would be staying. Mrs. DeJarnett simply commented that we would visit but could do so as long as we wanted.

After lunch, Mrs. DeJarnett helped us into our coats and hats, and we made our way through the deep snow to a large barn, which was located quite a distance behind the house. It was the biggest barn I had ever seen!

As we approached the entrance, Mrs. DeJarnett had us wait while she pushed a huge door to the side, revealing several cattle inside. I had never seen so many cows up close, and I was afraid, insisting she carry me. Mrs. DeJarnett carried me to another door and set me inside a small room where the cow feed was stored.

Moving from the barn, we were taken to see the chickens in the chicken house on a hillside beside the barn. After gathering eggs, we left the chickens and headed down the hill toward the barn once again. It was getting colder by that time, and we were all ready to go back to the house.

Back inside the house, Mrs. DeJarnett told us that her daughter, Judy, would be getting home from school very soon and that we needed to hide to surprise her when she walked into the house. At the sound of the school bus stopping in front of the house, Steve and I quickly found hiding places in the downstairs bedroom. When Judy came in, we both jumped out to surprise her. She was an eighth grader with dark, neck-length hair and a few freckles, and she seemed quite pleased to meet us.

Once Judy got settled in from school, Mrs. DeJarnett said that we were all going to go visit the neighbor lady across the road. Bundling up again, we set off to see Mrs. Swann. Although she was of no family relation, she was lovingly referred to as Aunt Versie. As we made our way up the road a little way, over a bridge, and across a small field, we began the ascent to a white two-story house at the top of the hill. Although there was a good path to walk on, the snow made it a difficult climb. Along the way, I announced to Judy that we were going to be staying with them for a visit. She seemed pleased, but she said little in response.

Reaching the top of the hill, we climbed onto Aunt Versie's long front porch. She was an elderly lady with glasses, and her hair was wrapped in a tightly tied scarf. She opened her arms for us to come to her and welcomed us to her home. Once inside, we warmed by the stove and were given more hot chocolate and offered some candy, which had apparently been left over from Christmas.

As evening drew near, Mrs. DeJarnett told us that Mr. DeJarnett would be coming home very soon. I'm not sure where he had been all this time, but he was most likely in the little community of Salt Rock, visiting some other farmers as they gathered at the local feed and seed hardware store. Again, we were encouraged to hide and surprise him when he came in the house. We did—and he was. Mr. DeJarnett was of medium height and a somewhat plump build. He held the stub of a cigar in his teeth, giving off a very distinctive, somewhat pungent odor. After meeting us, he went into the living room, sat down in his red vinyl easy chair, and read the evening paper. I climbed onto his lap and curled up close to him, cigar, and all.

This first day in the home of Scott, Alcie, and Judy DeJarnett proved to be the beginning of a six-and-a-half-year visit, which has affected my life to this very day.

CHAPTER 3

THE VISIT CONTINUES

The first few months with the DeJarnetts were exciting ones, and we met more members of the family. It did not take me very long to adjust to my new surroundings and to my new foster parents: Scott and Alcie DeJarnett. Within weeks, Mommy and Daddy replaced calling them Mr. and Mrs. DeJarnett. Judy was now our sister, and we had several cousins, aunts, and uncles, and two grandmas! Steve was a little slower to adjust and experienced some difficulty settling in at Salt Rock Elementary School. He eventually became used to our new home and was more settled at school.

Growing up on the farm was typical of farm life. There were beef cattle, which I became used to and was happy to be among without fear, chickens, which never seemed to get used to me reaching under them to steal their eggs, hogs, which I eventually claimed as pets, a collie named King, some wild farm cats, and some rabbits.

During that winter, I discovered the excitement of trudging through deep snow to the top of a hill and gliding quickly downward on Judy's sled. We found that the best way to pick up speed going down the hill was to grease the runners with fresh bacon fat. Let me give an example of the snow fun we enjoyed. To one side of the house, a small field was bordered by a creek. Just a few feet beyond the creek, a barbed wire fence ran along the bottom of a very steep hillside. Get the picture? We would make our way to the top of the hill and make a quick descent on our sled. By the time we got to the bottom, and having attained maximum speed, the trick was to either stop or roll off the sled before getting to the barbed wire fence. Sometimes we made it, but other times …

In addition to the store-bought sled, Daddy built a homemade wooden sled for us to ride as he pulled it behind his tractor. The roads were often frozen over, and Daddy would tow us up and down the icy road. It was great! We later figured out that the wooden sled was just as good on the hillsides as the store-bought one. Guiding that sled was a trick, however, since there were no moveable runners with which to guide it. We discovered that a hard lean to the left or right would turn the sled enough, depending upon how soon you began to lean.

Hot chocolate, homemade doughnuts, peanut butter fudge, homemade fruitcake, and fresh sausage and eggs were all part of our growing up in winter. Christmastime was especially fun. Each December, Judy, Steve, and I would trek through the snow to our neighbor's property in search of a Christmas tree. It seemed that Mr. Johnson had the most trees. When I think about it, I don't recall ever asking him if we could cut down a tree. We just did it. He knew it, of course, but he never complained or objected.

We would bring our Christmas tree home, and Daddy would saw off a flat edge on the trunk and nail it to a homemade tree stand. All of us helped with the multicolored lights, the glass ornaments of all shapes and colors, the icicles, and—best of all—a tree topper. Each year, I thought there could be no prettier tree than ours. I would lay on the couch or on the floor and just stare at it. The light given off by the gas stove in the living room, along with the lights of the tree, created a warm and peaceful feeling of being at home. Adding to the colorful Christmas tree, Daddy always framed the front porch roof with colored lights—the big outdoor kind—creating a colorful glow in the snow on the ground and on the large, snowcapped pine shrubs along the front sidewalk.

One of the most memorable Christmases was the year I realized that Santa was much closer to home than I had previously realized. Allow me to explain. While playing around the barn one day, fairly close to Christmas, Steve made a great discovery. In one of the side wings of the barn, there was a large wooden box where the winter supply of oats was stored. We loved to play in that oat box, burying one another in the oats and wrestling in it. That year, we discovered Santa had come early—and left our toys in the oats. We were delighted and could not help ourselves from taking a quick peek. Opening some of the packages was not too difficult. Making them *look unopened* was! Of course, we were found out, dampening Christmas day fun. By the way, that was the year I got my first bike and the year that Steve and I shared our first very own store-bought Champion brand metal runner sled.

During the winter months, Steve and I enjoyed working with Daddy in the barn. We took turns getting up at six o'clock and accompanying him to the barn to help feed the cattle. There was something special about getting up early, going to the hayloft to throw down bales of hay, and then tossing the hay into the mangers with a pitchfork. There were many chores to be done during those cold months. The chores included cleaning out the barn on a regular basis. Again, I don't wish to be crude, but there is only one way to describe this task.

With shovels and pitchforks, we would toss the "stuff" into the "stuff-spreader." When it was full, the tractor pulled the spreader out to fertilize the fields. The fun was in riding in the spreader as the stuff was being spread about. Of course, we were not allowed back into the house until we had shed our "stuffy" clothes and removed our "stuffy" shoes. Even at that, a much-needed bath was always in order. Other regular chores included cleaning out the rabbit pens, grinding corn into feed and carrying it to the feed bin, feeding the chickens in the chicken house, and various other small jobs.

Along with the farm chores, there was always time for play. The barn loft, filled with bales of hay, was perfect for building forts and creating tunnels leading to each one. One could easily go into a tunnel and move throughout the loft without ever being detected. Within the tunnel system, we created escape routes by moving one bale of hay in each tunnel. The escape routes also served as pop-up holes amid corncob battles. Looking back, I have often considered that God was watching over us with His protective hand as we played on that farm. Some of the games we played could have resulted in great injury.

Take the corncob battles, for example. We would break a corncob from field corn in half and insert three chicken or pigeon feathers into the soft core of the cob. Those corncob darts would fly straighter and hit harder with the feathers inserted. While it was great fun throwing them at each other in the hay forts but getting hit with one of those projectiles was another matter. Ouch!

With the arrival of spring, and the cattle returned to the pastures, it was time for plowing and planting. Daddy would get his plow, roller, and disc reworked and ready for the fields. I loved to follow along behind the plow in the newly overturned dirt. There was something truly special about the feel of freshly plowed dirt on my bare feet—not to mention the unique odor of freshly turned soil. The plowing and disking were always followed by the planting of field corn, sweet corn (for eating), popcorn, and oats. Along with the planting of large fields was the garden planting of green beans, radishes, cabbage, lettuce, peas, Irish potatoes, sweet potatoes, and kale greens.

One of the highlights of spring and early summer was strawberry season. Mom loved to plant and pick strawberries. In fact, she loved it so much that she had as many as four patches at any given time. When I say patches, I do not mean little twenty-by-twenty-feet areas. Our strawberry patches were strawberry fields. Steve and I would help fill a crate of twenty-four quarts, which always seemed nearly impossible. We managed though, amid all of my griping about sweat, beestings, and the hot weather. There was a silver lining in this hard work, however. We sold the strawberries as a means of making extra money. Steve and I had our own strawberry stand, making our own extra money.

After the strawberries were gone, blackberry season came in and were ready for picking. Most blackberries grow in the wild, and ours were located at the "head of the holler," as we would say. In preparation to go blackberry pickin', we would don long pants and long-sleeved shirts to avoid getting "chiggers." There were also snakes to be on the lookout for. The usual time to hit the blackberry patches was in the early morning while the ground was still wet with dew.

Armed with our two-quart lard buckets and a couple of two-gallon galvanized buckets, we would make our way to the head of the holler. After what often seemed like hours with the sun growing hotter, and with the buckets filled with fresh, plump blackberries, we would make our way back to the house complete with berry-stained hands and mouths. The reward for picking the strawberries and blackberries was the jams, jellies, and preserves that Mom Alcie would make and can for the coming months.

At this point, allow me to digress and talk a little more about my foster sister, Judy. It seems that Judy and I always had a great "little brother-big sister" relationship. Among the more outstanding special memories was the day Judy decided she wanted to take me to school with her during eighth grade. This meant getting to ride the school bus, which was another first. Upon arriving at school, I was taken to a classroom of second graders. The teacher was quite nice and offered a picture for me to color, but I was too shy to go to her desk and get it.

Then, there were those special times when Judy needed a dance partner to practice the latest dance moves as seen on *American Bandstand*. It was either her bedpost or me as her dance partner, and I was more fun. Judy also tried to teach me how to ride a bicycle, and she even let me use her bike. I was a little slow with that because the bike was too big, and I ended up pushing the bike more than riding it.

Now, having said all of that about Judy, let me give you a *realistic* picture of our big sister and little brother relationship. One afternoon, Judy had been working diligently putting together one of those Chef Boyardee pizza mixes. She had completed the assembly of her homemade treat, leaving it sitting on the counter while the oven heated.

In the meanwhile, I had been playing on the kitchen floor and noticed a fly buzzing around the kitchen. Judy did not seem to notice the little bugger flyin' around, and I considered it my duty to guard her culinary masterpiece. Just as that fly was about to land, I managed to grab the flyswatter and smash him right in the middle of Chef Boyardee! Judy heard the *splat*, turning just in time to see the kill—and that was exactly what she wanted to do at that very moment! She was so angry that she couldn't think of anything to say or do, so she just let out a resounding "God bless America!" of which Kate Smith would have been proud.

As Judy was proclaiming her patriotic spirit, Mom came into the kitchen. "What is going on?"

Without missing a beat, Judy cried out, "That brat ruined my pizza!"

What can I say? I was only trying to help.

The summer months were filled with playing out in the pastures, deep in the woods, and in the vacant barn. Once our chores were completed, the day was ours. I now realize how much God's hand was upon us, as Steve and I played all over that farm. Let me give you a couple of examples.

I do not remember this, but Mom Alcie related the story to me on numerous occasions. It seems that Steve and I were playing on the hill behind the house one morning. As lunchtime drew near, Mom Alcie rang the large dinner bell for us to come in and eat. Steve showed up, but I was not with him. After waiting for a little bit, Mom rang the bell and called for me again. No answer. She felt it was time to interrogate Steve as to my whereabouts. With a bit of coaxing—probably on the threat of a good whipping—he told her where I was. It seems that we had been playing cowboys and Indians. Making her way to one of the far pasture fields, Mom Alcie found me tied to a tree, just "a squallin'," as she put it. Who knows how long I had been tied to that tree!

On another occasion, we were playing in the empty hayloft where some loose hay was still lying around. As we played, I wandered to the front of the loft, which had a window opening overlooking the area in front of the barn. Just beneath the window was a small, two-feet-square opening in the floor of the loft. There was some loose hay covering the opening, and when I stepped onto the loose hay, I fell through to the concrete floor below. The fall would not have been so bad except for the fact that there was a mowing machine parked just beneath. When I fell, I landed on the mowing machine, bouncing from it onto the concrete floor. Fortunately, I wasn't hurt and just had the breath knocked out of me for a while. Again, God was watching over me.

On still another occasion, I was with Dad as he went to check the watering trough in one of the pastures for the cattle. We came to the trough where some of the cattle were gathered. We had to move them out of the way to get to the trough. All was going well until I decided to move Shorty out of the way. Shorty was the bull among the cattle, and he was extremely "contrary," as Dad would put it. I called him mean—and he was.

As I tried to chase the bull out of the way, he turned on me and began chasing me. I took off down the hill toward a fence as fast as I could run. However, just shy of the fence, I tripped and fell. Shorty was still coming after me. Daddy, having seen the situation, ran after the quickly approaching bull, trying to head him off before he got to me. I do not believe I had ever seen Dad move that quickly before. He was able to head Shorty off and club him with the heavy walking stick he always carried out in the pastures. Once again, God was watching over me.

Sundays were always special days, and they began early. Steve or I would race to the paper box to get the Sunday paper.

Whoever got to the paper box first had dibs on the funnies. I remember lying on the front porch with the comic section spread out before me as I carefully tried to figure out who Dick Tracy was going after next or what kind of trouble Beetle Bailey was getting into with the Sarge. Around nine, Mom would call us in to get ready for Sunday school and church.

I always enjoyed going to Sunday school and church, especially my first primary class with Mrs. Ray. Osel Perry, a neighbor not far from our house, taught the intermediate boys' class. Even sitting in the preaching service was fun when I watched the preacher and listened to his fervent, if not animated, sermons.

Enon Baptist Church, a small country church, was about a mile up the road from our house. That was where I first began to sense God's dealing with me about my salvation. I remember sitting in revival services and watching as people would respond to the invitation to receive Christ. My first serious thoughts about my spiritual condition came when Judy became a Christian.

I was not in church the day Judy was "saved," but I remember the discussion around the house and the Sunday afternoon she was baptized in Lambert's Creek. Having no baptistry inside the small church, all baptisms were conducted either in a local river or—as in this case)—in a dammed-up creek on the Lambert's farm. It was then that I began to give more thought about my own need to be saved, although I did not realize all that was involved in such a decision. Up to that time, no one had shared with me what was needed in order to be saved.

Ruth Ann, a neighbor girl my age, was saved during a revival meeting. I was in that service, and for whatever reason, I was greatly impacted by her decision. In fact, the following day at school, I asked her about what she had done. I don't really recall her response, but she realized she was "lost" and needed to be saved.

Osel Perry was my Sunday School teacher, but he was more than that. It seems that Osel took a special interest in Steve and me—just as he did with most of the kids living along Tyler Creek Road. On many Sunday mornings, Steve and I would hurry to get dressed for church in order to leave early enough to accompany Osel as he walked to church. We always enjoyed walking and talking with him along the way.

I grew quite attached to Osel and made it a point to sit with him during the Sunday morning worship services. Ours being a small country church, there was no *formal* choir. My uncle Lyle was the choir director, and every Sunday morning, he issued a call to those in the congregation: "Y'all, come on up here and help us sing this morning." Osel was always a part of the choir, and I felt that my place was right beside him in the back row.

Although I felt very much at home and a part of the DeJarnett family during those six and a half years, I would sometimes raise questions about my "real" mother and father. This bothered me from time to time, especially, about my last name: Ying. I was constantly reminded that it was Chinese and that my father was Chinese. Sometimes, kids at school would tease me about my last name, commenting that I didn't "look" Chinese, although some said my eyes did have a certain Chinese look about them.

Mom Alcie was always good about answering me with whatever information she had been given, as sparse as it was. All we knew was our mother's name and that she had left Steve and me with a babysitter—supposedly for a few days—and never returned. Who *was* this babysitter? Where did she live? These questions flashed across my mind, but they remained unanswered for many years. As for our real father, we were told his name was Jack Ying.

During some of our conversations with Mom Alcie, Steve would say that he remembered our mother, describing her as very pretty and having black hair. He even recalled such details as eating oatmeal from pie pans. Beyond that, there was no information about our parents or the first four years of our lives. So, for the time being, we would have to be satisfied with limited information about our "real" parents.

I have pointed all of these things out to provide you a brief glimpse of the loving care, satisfaction, and joy Steve and I experienced living with the DeJarnetts. They were our family. Those years were some of the most important of my life, as God used them to form my basic values and outlook on life. All the aforementioned accounts did not happen by mere happenstance. It was all a part of God's plan for us, which had been set in motion that January day when Steve and I were moved from the Lewis home to the DeJarnett home.

On a side note—but very importantly—I need to let you know about a significant relational change that occurred during our stay with the DeJarnetts. As you will recall, the social worker assigned to Steve and me was Mrs. Morgan. Upon her leaving the Department of Welfare, we were under the watchful eye of Mrs. Abraham for a short time.

One afternoon, upon arriving home from school, we noticed an unfamiliar car parked in the driveway. As we entered the back door, Mom Alcie introduced us to a new social worker. Mrs. Ruth Manley appeared to us a total stranger, but we soon learned that she had known us for several years—even predating our stay with the Lewis family in Milton. With a certain tone of excitement, she immediately said, "Jimmy, I've known you since you were about this big." She positioned her arms and hands like she was holding an infant.

As it turned out, she was the very first social worker assigned to Steve and me. Because of that, Mrs. Manley had knowledge of my first four years and the background from which I came from birth—a knowledge of facts she would never share with Steve or me.

I've often thought about how wonderful God is for putting the right people in our paths at the right times. This foundation would later give me the strength to survive.

CHAPTER 4

THE VISIT COMES
TO AN END

Someone once said, "All good things must come to an end."
Well, I believe there is an element of truth to that adage, and so
it was with the "visit" in the home of Scott and Alcie DeJarnett.
It took me many years to come to an acceptable understanding
of why the change was made, and I still often wonder what
might have been the outcome had we remained in that home.
Change, however, is often a great part of living, and we are
called upon to accept and adapt to the changes we encounter
along the way.

I really do not recall how the news was broken to Steve
and me that we would be leaving the DeJarnett home. Mrs.
Manley unexpectedly visited our house one day—with the
news that we would be paying a visit to a new home where
we would meet a nice couple. This really wasn't anything new
for us since we had done it twice before while living with the
DeJarnetts. On those other occasions, we had been taken
for weekend visits with other families. For varying reasons,
neither of those previous weekend visits resulted in leaving the
DeJarnetts' home. From those visits, we began to get the idea
that it was a very real possibility that we would be moved again
to another home.

This third time, however, there was something different about the visit. For one thing, this visit was *not* a weekend visit. We were taken to a small, rural home in Wayne County, where we were introduced to Charles "Charlie" and Phyllis Martin. This couple was younger than Mom Alcie and Poppy Scott DeJarnett, and they gladly welcomed us into their home. The Martin house, being a one-story house, was quite a change from our house in Salt Rock, and the room in which Steve and I would possibly be sleeping was drastically smaller.

I do not recall the initial part of this meeting, but I do recall the personal time we spent with Charlie. While Phyllis Martin and Mrs. Manley visited, Charlie had Steve and me climb into his 1957 Ford, which was complete with fender skirts and Continental kit on the back. We drove around the countryside for what seemed to be quite a long time as he told us what we could expect should we come live with them. This was *totally* different from other visits we had made. It began to sound as though the decision had already been made. The more I heard, the more anxious I became about this potential move. It had the sound of a perpetual vacationland. Steve, on the other hand, was his usual overly cautious self about the matter and said nothing.

Having spent most of the afternoon with the Martins, we made our way back home. During the drive back to Salt Rock,

Mrs. Manley asked us what we thought about the visit with the Martins and what would we think about being moved to their home. I immediately told her that I would like the move, but Steve remained less enthusiastic about it.

The decision was made. We would be leaving the DeJarnetts to live with the Martins. That night was one I will never forget. As we lay in our beds, I heard Steve crying. I asked him what was wrong, and his response still rings in my ears and breaks my heart to this day: "It's all your fault!" he said. "You just had to tell Mrs. Manley we wanted to move. Well, I don't want to leave!"

For the first time, I truly realized how much a part of our lives this home had become, and, in truth, I really did not want to leave either. I lay there thinking about the past six and a half years and all the wonderful times we had had—and now it was all going to end. I tried to put that out of my mind and turned my thoughts to the seemingly wonderful life Charlie Martin had described during our ride through the countryside, but it really didn't help.

The date was set when we would be leaving our home in Salt Rock and moving to Lavalette, Wayne County. It was a hot day on June 22, 1962, when the move was made. As I think back to that day, I do not recall any excitement about the move. It just wasn't there. I do not even recall the first day in the Martin home—like I do our first day in the DeJarnett home. It simply was not the same.

Our lives had been turned upside down. There was no large farmland on which to roam. Most of our indoor time was spent in our bunk beds, having no floor space in our room on which to play. As far as outdoor play went, there was not any. The area of what should have been a yard was still like an unimproved lot wrought with rocks and uneven landscaping that was quite overgrown with weeds. A series of wooden planks served as the sidewalk from the road to the front door of the house. The backyard area was not much better. The reality was that we were living with total strangers in an unfamiliar and drastically different environment.

There were some new things I did find interesting because I had never seen them before. Whereas Mom Alcie used a gas range on which to cook, this house was all electric. For the first time, I saw an electric range. I remember it well because of the terrific burn I sustained from it. While looking at it one afternoon, I asked Mrs. Martin about it, and she explained how it worked. What I did not realize was that when the elements were turned off and appeared to no longer be hot, they definitely were! They weren't red, and I put my hand on one of the elements. It was great lesson there to keep your hands off the stove—even if it looks cool!

September came, and we were enrolled in our new school. I was in the sixth grade, and Steve was in the eighth grade. During my first five school years, I had seen "new kids" at our school, but I never thought too much about how *they* felt about their new surroundings. Now, *I* was the new kid, and I did not like it at all—and I did not like the school building. The old, run-down building did not even have a gymnasium, a playground, or a cafeteria.

My teacher, Mrs. Hale, was certainly nice enough, but it took a bit more time for the classmates to warm up to me— and me to them. I did settle in and became more comfortable in the class. As the year progressed, however, things turned for the worse. It was my conduct that was the issue. I was quite hyper and, apparently, a challenge to Mrs. Hale. She had a system for maintaining order in her classroom that involved having the student's name written on the blackboard when that student misbehaved. There were hash marks after the name for each additional offense. At the end of the week, a special work assignment was given to those students for the weekend. My name constantly appeared on the board—along with several hash marks.

Then, it happened. I experienced a rude awakening to the seriousness of my poor deportment. I will summarize that abrupt realization by relating a conversation between two teachers, which I happened to overhear one day during the lunch hour. I had been playing outside and came to the front double doors of the building. It was normal for teachers to be standing in the hallway at the school entrance to keep watch over the students at lunch. As I approached the doorway, I overheard Mrs. Hale talking about the bad conduct of a student, and, that if things did not change, she was going to transfer that student to the basement sixth grade class.

The other teacher said, "Mrs. Hale, who is this student?"

What came next nearly floored me.

"Jimmy Martin!" she replied.

Who is Jimmy Martin? In short, it was me! When we moved in with the Martins, we assumed their last name to keep from having to explain our given last name to people. It was a matter of convenience. When I heard *my* name, I was shocked that I was not liked by my teacher. Worse yet, I was probably going to be sent to the class where all hard-to-deal-with sixth grade students were sent: Mrs. Shoemate's class. Thankfully, my deportment did improve, and I managed to remain in Mrs. Hale's class for the rest of the year.

CHAPTER 5

BEHIND CLOSED DOORS

"No one really knows what goes on behind closed doors." There is great truth to that saying, which you will understand in this chapter. This is a new and different chapter of a story, and it represents a totally new and different chapter in the lives of two young boys. We had grown accustomed to the security and the warmth of the loving family we had previously known.

What was going on behind the closed doors of this new home was another matter. Let me take you back to the first weeks with the Martins. This home was much different, but it was bearable—for a while. Then, one afternoon, we heard a knock on the door. Charlie Martin answered the door, and as he opened the door, I saw Daddy DeJarnett standing there. I wanted to run out and hug him, but I was not allowed to do so or even be seen from the door. As I learned in later years, Scott DeJarnett had come by to drop off some of our things that had been left at their house, and he was apparently hoping to see Steve and me again.

Once more, I realized what I had left when the move was made to live with the Martins. This was *not* my home. My home was in Salt Rock with the DeJarnetts. From that point until the day, I left the Martins' home, I regretted the decision I had made. I really don't want to go into detail about events that occurred at the Martin home, but it is important that I share some of them to show how God's hand remained with us—and how He looks after those who have seemingly been abandoned by those who love them and who they love.

Charlie Martin was a World War II veteran and a medically retired railroad worker. Due to an accident on the job, Charlie had one arm amputated just below the elbow. I mention this only because I honestly believe that Charlie's conduct and outlook on life stemmed from this terrible accident. Charlie was certainly more demanding toward Steve and me. He was stricter than Mom or Daddy DeJarnett had ever been, even though discipline was always a part of growing up in their home. With Charlie, though, something about his disciplinary actions was much different from that which we had been accustomed. In retrospect, I realize that it was his lack of genuine parental love for two young boys in need of love and acceptance and the discipline untempered by such parental love.

For Charlie, it seemed, having two foster children in the home simply meant providing a roof over their heads and food for their stomachs. Any parental relationship beyond that—aside from the monthly welfare checks—was never demonstrated. The father-son kinship we had known with Daddy DeJarnett was never evident with Charlie. It was as though we were perpetual "visitors" in the home but never actually a part of it.

There were occasions when Charlie needed to run into town for various items, and he would ask one or both of us to go along. We were always glad to ride somewhere, and we were always willing to go. What Charlie failed to mention was that on the way home, there was always one extra stop to make. You see, Charlie was an alcoholic, and that one little item was never detected by the State Welfare social worker).

On the way home from town, Charlie would pull into the parking lot of a little "beer garden," as it was called. Steve and I were never allowed to go inside the establishment, and we were told to wait in the car for Charlie to come out with his six-pack. Upon getting back inside the car, the odor coming from Charlie revealed that he had already been drinking. We were always instructed that Phyllis was not to know about this little stop or that he had been drinking with us riding in the car, but I'm sure she must have known, given the beer he kept in the refrigerator. That was another one of the changes in our home life to which we were not accustomed after living with the DeJarnetts.

Whenever Steve or I misbehaved, discipline was both deserved and meted out. It was the way it was executed that always troubled me more than the actual administration of it. First, Charlie was the administrator of punishment, which was usually inflicted after he had been drinking. For example, after announcing that I was going to be spanked, Charlie would send Steve to a small woodpile to bring back a small board that was suitable for the paddling. Steve somehow managed to bring back the smallest board he thought he could get away with, and usually, after the first several whacks, it would break. That did not deter Charlie. He just found another one.

What I am about to share at this point, I do so with a certain amount of reluctance, as some deep-seated emotions arise. However, I know that if I am to tell the story, I must tell *all* of it in order that you might better understand the greatness and goodness of God toward those who are unable to protect themselves, especially young children. At that point, Steve was an eighth grader—and I was in the sixth grade.

We did not live on a farm like we had in Salt Rock, but Charlie raised hogs with Phyllis's uncle John Porter. Next to the hog pen, old food scraps, "pig slop," were stored in a large fifty-gallon metal barrel. During the winter months, this barrel would often freeze over.

January 24, 1963, was a particularly cold morning—I remember the date because it was my twelfth birthday—and Charlie decided that the barrel needed to be thawed out. The temperatures had been unusually cold, and on that morning, the temperature was around fifteen to sixteen below zero. Nevertheless, Charlie insisted that the barrel needed to be thawed out that morning.

Steve and I were given this task, and we set off to do it while Charlie drove away. The problem was starting the fire underneath the barrel since there was a constant wind blowing, and all we had were some matches and wood from the woodpile. After many unsuccessful attempts to start the fire, and with numbness setting in on our hands and feet, we decided that the only way to start this fire was to get some gasoline and douse the wood. When Steve went to Uncle John Porter's store, just across the road, John's wife, Dessie, asked what the gas was for. Steve told her, and Aunt Dessie took us back to our house— only to discover that both of us had experienced mild cases of frostbite on our feet.

Charlie was still not home when we were taken inside, but his mother-in-law happened to be spending the day there since Phyllis was in the hospital to deliver her baby. Inside the house, Phyllis's mom realized the situation and immediately took steps to treat the problem. We survived that painful afternoon, but we were not allowed to go back to that barrel.

After getting well settled from the morning issue with the barrel, Dessie Porter called and asked me to come up to their house. When I arrived at Dessie's house, she greeted me by singing "Happy Birthday" in her rough, shrill, piercing voice.

It was a welcome sound because I knew that both John and Dessie Porter loved us. They knew what life was like for us in the Martin home.

Aunt Dessie, as she became known to me, handed a small gift to me. I opened the gift and pulled out a brand-new black Bible. It was my very first Bible. I had been given the *Gideon New Testament* in the fifth grade, but I had never had a full Bible. I was so proud of this gift. Aunt Dessie wrote inside the front and back covers: "To Jimmie, From Aunt Dessie and Uncle John, January 24, 1963." That meant everything to me. I still have that Bible, and I look it at every now and then as a reminder of God's presence and watchful care.

Later that afternoon, Charlie returned home to discover that the barrel had not been thawed out. To make matters worse, I had even gone to Aunt Dessie's for a birthday party when I was supposed to be working on that barrel. I'm not sure which made Charlie the maddest: not thawing out the barrel or Aunt Dessie giving me the birthday party and gift, which he tried to make me give back.

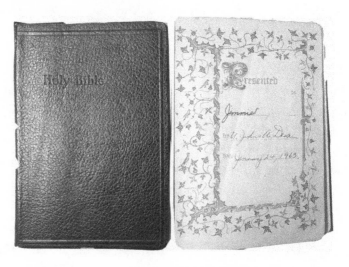

What I am about to share with you has never been openly shared with anyone, and it is the most difficult part of this story. During the time that Phyllis was in the hospital, Steve and I were alone with Charlie at night. During that time, I was sexually abused by Charlie on several occasions. In those days, such things were *not* openly talked about—not even with our social worker and especially not with Charlie's wife. I will not go into any more detail about those experiences. I include the experience simply to clarify the nature of the environment in which we were living.

Allow me to step aside a moment and tell you more about Aunt Dessie Porter. She was definitely one of a kind, and I liked her very much. She was always kind and loving, and she made me feel like very much a part of her and Uncle John's life. The Porters took Steve and me to church on Sundays at the Macedonia Baptist Church. I still remember sitting in the preaching service and listening to Aunt Dessie's shrill, raspy voice rising above everybody as we would sing the hymns. I imagine that everyone knew when Dessie Porter wasn't there. The singing just was not quite the same. I imagine that some would say, "Thankfully!"

During those Sunday services, I was spiritually influenced. My Sunday school class was a good class, and our teacher was a kind and thoughtful man. He always talked to us about being saved, but the pastor impressed me the most. I was always amazed by how well he knew the Bible. The way he would quote passages from memory astounded me. I always took my Bible and looked them up to see if he was right, and he always was. I realize that might not sound like much, but to a twelve-year-old boy, it was impressive. As a preacher of God's Word now, I seek to know from memory the passages I preach—or

at the very least be so familiar with them that I can make eye
contact with the congregants as I read passages.

One other memory about those Sundays has always stood
out in my mind. One Sunday afternoon, Uncle John, Aunt
Dessie, and I attended a baptism service in a large stream near
the church. What impressed me the most was the comment
the pastor made as he prepared to baptize a nine-year-old or
a ten-year-old. He said something to the effect that "Today, I
have the privilege to do something that only pastors have at
some point in their ministry: to baptize their own children."
The pastor was about to baptize his own son. That seemed
so special to me, and I never had any idea that I too would
someday share in that same privilege twice.

By late spring of 1963, Steve and I managed to endure the
Martins—until one very bad day. I do not even recall what
precipitated the event, but I was about to be punished for
something that had displeased Charlie. Steve was sent to get
a suitable board, but this time, he refused. This made Charlie
even angrier, and he threatened Steve.

Steve ran to the phone, called our social worker, Mrs.
Manley, and said, "Get us out of here!"

The phone was taken from him and hung up immediately.
This got Mrs. Manley's attention. She showed up at our school
the very next afternoon. Once inside her car, Mrs. Manley
asked us what was going on.

We had had visits along the way with Mrs. Manley, but
we had always told her that everything was just fine. I really
cannot tell you why we always lied about the situation—
except that we feared getting into trouble with Charlie. Well,
this time, we didn't care. We wanted to tell the story and get
out of that house—and so we did! Both of us opened up to
everything, well, nearly everything. I still did not tell her about

the sexual abuse because, again, there wasn't any such thing at that time—at least not in open discussion.

Regardless, Mrs. Manley took us home and sat down with the Martins. Steve and I were sent outside. The next several weeks at the Martins were filled with tension, as one might expect, but on June 13, 1963, we were removed from that house to live in another foster home. We had been delivered from our worst experience. That was another example that God is, indeed, a deliverer and protector for the weak.

CHAPTER 6

THE DELIVERANCE

The first time I met Robert and Anna Lou Means in June of 1963 was in the West Virginia State Welfare Department office at the county courthouse in Huntington. It was, by then, a familiar setting. Steve and I had been there many times for occasional checkups on how things were going in the foster home. The staff was always so loving and warm toward us. This time, however, we were there to meet potential foster parents. We met Mr. Means first, and then we were introduced to his wife, Anna Lou.

The passing years have clouded my memory about that first visit, but I do remember it was a pleasant and welcome change. Mr. Means was an attorney in Huntington, and Mrs. Means was a stay-at-home mom with their two children, Lou Anne, a fourth grader, and Kevin, a first grader. I do remember the anticipation I sensed as we prepared to move. The wait seemed quite long, but moving day finally came. Steve and I were introduced to our new home on East Pea Ridge, which was not far from Barboursville, West Virginia.

This house was located on a private drive containing only five homes. Trees lined each side of the road, which created a kind of canopy over the road. As we came close to the end of Mahood Drive, I noticed a three-foot rock wall to my left, bordering the yard with tall pine trees growing along the full length of the wall. At each end of the stone wall, there were entrances leading from the main drive to the house. The first entrance was a stone walkway up the hill to the left side of the house, and the second was the driveway, leading to the right side of the house. Each entrance was marked by a stone column about six or seven feet high at the end of the wall. Atop each column was a four-sided light, the kind used as signal lights on railroads, each side displaying a different color when lit.

The house, known as Hilltop Manor, was a two-story structure with three main sections. The two-story center section had four columns at the front entrance and a chimney on the left side of the main entrance. The roof of the porch entrance was a sundeck extending from an A-frame portion of the second story. An American flag was waving from the front of the A-frame entrance into the second story.

To the left of the main section, there was a single-story wing or extension of the main house. To the right of the main area, there was another single-story wing with a large bay window in the center and another chimney at that end. This wing section was the den. *The den?* I had heard of houses having a den, but that was on TV and *not* in real life. The front yard was large, extending about thirty to thirty-five yards down the hill to Mahood Drive. The back of the house was three levels with the basement being the ground floor.

Once inside, we were given the grand tour and shown the room where we would be staying. It was a large room with twin beds. Another bedroom was located at the top of the staircase toward the back of the house, and French doors opened to the sundeck over the front entrance.

Downstairs was equally fascinating to me. The den had a rustic look with stained wooden walls and a fireplace at one end. The bay window looked out toward the driveway. I won't go any further into the layout of the house, except to say that it seemed huge.

It didn't take long to get settled in and begin to feel like a part of the family. Lou Anne, Kevin, and I hit it off well from the very start. Steve and Kevin did quite well, but there was a bit of friction between Steve and Lou Anne. Up until then, she had been the oldest child, but now she was bumped back to number three.

The week after we moved in, Mrs. Means informed us that we were going to the pool for the afternoon, which became the daily routine for the next three weeks or so. Life that summer was one of much relaxation and enjoyment. I remember commenting to Mrs. Means that I felt like I was on vacation, and I had never even *been* on one, which leads me to another new experience.

Mr. Means' parents lived in western Kentucky, near the Kentucky Lake and Dam at Paducah. Plans were made to travel with Mrs. Means' parents (the Mays) to Paducah, which meant an eight-hour drive and a week stay in a lake resort. It was probably the most exciting thing I had ever experienced. Just the anticipation of the vacation kept me going "on all cylinders," probably to the point of being nearly annoyingly unbearable to everyone else.

I remember the first time I saw one of the large lakes in western Kentucky. Lou Anne had told me that the water was blue, but I could not conceive of it until I saw it as we crossed that first large span over the water. I could not take my eyes off it. That week was great, and we met two new "grandparents." I had never learned how to swim but was determined to learn by the end of the week. With a lot of encouragement and much-needed support, literally, from Mr. Mays, I did learn to swim a little bit—even if it was only dogpaddling.

Arriving back home, we settled more into a routine as members of the Means family. By the end of the summer, I had met and become very good friends with a neighbor boy, Eddie Meade. Our houses were separated by some trees, a white corral-type fence, and a path leading to their house. Eddie became a regular visitor at our house, as I did at his.

The rest of the summer was spent taking swimming lessons, spending weekends on the Ohio River aboard our houseboat, and learning how to ride horses and how to care for them. While I was familiar with caring for farm animals, I had no experience in caring for horses. As it happened, the Means had three horses and one burro. I soon learned how to care for them, and I eventually served as the groom, brushing them down and washing them in preparation for horse shows. Lou Anne was an accomplished equestrian, having won many ribbons and trophies.

I eventually began attending the Pea Ridge Baptist Church and making new friends. I was introduced to the church by attending vacation Bible school. That was the first time I recall ever attending VBS. The church also sponsored a Boy Scout troop. Eddie introduced me to scouting and helped me work on my steps for Tenderfoot and Second Class. My brief experience with scouting was truly enjoyable, and I learned tying knots, camping, hiking, and building campfires.

As summer passed, plans for beginning the new school year at Barboursville Junior High School were made. The school was very nice, and it was much larger than my previous school. I felt out of place at first, but I soon settled in, quite often giving some of my teachers fits with my hyperactivity. I was not a particularly good student, but I had fun. By the middle of the school year, I had made quite a name for myself among some of the teachers.

The teacher I think I most frustrated was Mr. Henry France. He was a nice man, and he was actually a pretty good science teacher. I really could have learned a lot from him if I had not been so busy creating havoc along with my new friend and cohort in adolescent behavior, Timmy Meade. We were the twosome of the seventh grade: Tim Meade and Jim Means.

Oh, yes! For the second time, Steve and I assumed the name of our foster parents. This time, however, I occasionally ran into someone who had known me while living in one of our previous foster homes. Since it was commonplace among teenagers to call each other by their last name, it was always interesting—if not confusing—when a former acquaintance would call out, "Hey, Ying, what's up?" or, "Hey, Martin, how's it goin'?" The look on my current friends' faces was always fun to watch—and even more fun to explain. By that time, the purpose of taking on the family name of foster parents to avoid confusion had backfired.

I can sum up my hyper classroom behavior by relating one experience in Mr. France's science class. As in any school, there are those students who stand out because of their incorrigible behavior. Among those incorrigibles at Barboursville Junior High were Benny, Allen, and Andy (last names intentionally omitted). On that day, I had been especially hyperactive in science class. Having tried to deal with me in several ways, and after various threats along the line of being "severely thrashed," Mr. France finally ceded defeat when he told me—in front of the whole class—that he would rather have three Bennys, two or three Allens, and two Andys than have one of me in his class. I had made the big-time! With the congratulatory affirmation from my cohort, Tim, I knew my reputation was secure.

Being a teacher myself, I now realize how the Lord was preparing me for what He had planned for me in the classroom *as* a teacher with so-called ADHD students in my classroom. I am rarely caught off guard by my students' behavior. God has allowed me to take my own adolescent experiences and use the wisdom gained to handle most situations. Even amid the confusion of that seventh-grade year, I was more settled than I had been during my sixth-grade year. My home life was a total positive contrast to that with the Martins, and thus, it was more secure, which brings me to a crucial turn in my adolescent life.

Eddie Meade and I became partners in a car-washing business. We combed most of the East Pea Ridge neighborhoods and offered to wash people's cars for pay. We walked everywhere we went, carrying our cleaning supplies with us.

While walking down the road one day, Eddie asked, "Are you a Christian?"

No one had asked me that before. I hadn't given any thought about becoming a Christian since attending the Macedonia Baptist Church with Aunt Dessie. I gave a flimsy response: "No. You?"

He responded by telling me that he had been baptized as a baby, making him a Christian. That had never happened to me and sounded quite strange. I passed it off for a while, but the Lord would not let that question get away from me. The more I thought about *not* being able to say a definite *yes,* the more uneasy I became. I decided that I wanted to become a Christian, but I really didn't know what to do.

During the early spring of 1964, the Lord began dealing with me more seriously, and every worship service caused me to feel very awkward, especially at the invitation to "receive Christ as Lord and Savior," given by the pastor at the conclusion of each service. I listened to Rev. Moore, but I heard no real answer about *what* I needed to do. Maybe he *did* explain it, but it never got through.

Finally, one week, I thought, "*This is it.*" At the very next Sunday service, I was going to do it—whatever *that* meant. I positioned myself strategically toward the front—about the fourth or fifth row—of the sanctuary. That would eliminate the long walk from the back of the sanctuary, where I normally sat with my friends. For whatever reason, I was able to talk Gary and Sharon into sitting up front with me that Sunday. I figure God moved them because no one else could get them out of the back section.

I need to point out that Gary and Sharon were already Christians. They had made that decision before I showed up at Pea Ridge. Since Gary had it all pretty much down pat, I figured he would be there to give me some encouragement in case I chickened out at the last minute.

The preacher preached—although I haven't a clue on what—the final hymn was being sung, the invitation time had begun, and my heart was pounding while I hung on to the pew in front of me. That's right, I was experiencing white-knuckle syndrome. Finally, I knew I had to move, but I needed a little encouragement. I turned to Gary and said, "Gary, I'm going forward. Will you go with me?"

"No."

No? Now is not the time to say no!

I was on my own, and time was growing short as the last verse was being sung. I mustered all the courage I could and stepped out. Reverend Moore greeted me at the front and asked if I was coming to be saved. I said, "Yes."

However, there was a problem. He introduced me as coming to receive Christ, but I had never even prayed—let alone asked Christ to save me. The church rejoiced with the official, if not obligatory, *amen*, and I walked out of there secure in the understanding that I was now a Christian.

All the way home, I began to wonder how I was going to break the news to Mr. and Mrs. Means that I was now a Christian and had "joined the church." The ten-minute walk home was enough time to work out my strategy for how to break the news. When I got home, I ran into Steve first thing and thought, "*Here's my chance to practice my presentation.*"

"Hey, Steve, guess what I did today?"

"What?"

"I joined the church, and I'm going to be baptized."

"You're kidding! Boy, are you in trouble!"

Wait a minute here. In trouble? For what? Aw, not to worry. He doesn't know about these things. It'll be just fine.

Sunday lunch was not the large family mealtime many families share after church. In fact, it was pretty much every person for himself.

As I was scrounging for some lunch in the kitchen, Mrs. Means came in.

"How was church?" she asked.

"Oh … fine, I guess. By the way, I joined the church this morning."

"You did *what*?"

I repeated my confession, quite alarmed at her response. *Where is the enthusiasm I had seen at the church? Why is she so upset?*

She continued, "You can't do that. You're not old enough to make that kind of decision or to know what you're doing—and, besides, you haven't even been to communicant classes yet!

Communicant classes? What the heck is that? No one said anything about going to school to join the church and become a Christian. Just when and where were these classes supposed to be held?

The next day, a call was made to Mrs. Manley—and I was told to explain to her what I had done at the church. I felt like I was in trouble, but I didn't really understand why. I made every effort to explain my action to Mrs. Manley. She was receptive, but equally as questioning as Mrs. Means had been. I didn't remember things being this complicated when Judy joined the church or when Ruth Ann Hicks became a Christian. I must have left out a step. I talked more to Mrs. Manley, and the church wanted to baptize me. I continued attending Pea Ridge Church, but I was *not* baptized. Why not? It's simple—the emergency appendectomy!

CHAPTER 7

A NEAR-DEATH EXPERIENCE

This is not about seeing a brilliant white light at the end of a long tunnel as I floated above my lifeless body. It *is* about the continual protective hand and watchful eye of a heavenly Father upon a child in great need of His presence. This thought will be continued later. For now, allow me to relate the event that did, in fact, bring me closer to death than I initially realized.

On a Sunday night in April 1964, I went to bed feeling somewhat uneasy in my stomach. I awoke the next morning feeling much worse. As usual, Steve and I were the only ones up at six, getting ready for school and grabbing a quick breakfast before walking to the school bus stop. I couldn't eat anything that morning and told Steve that I was sick, but he insisted that I would be all right and urged me on to school.

At school that morning, I was feeling gradually worse. I attended my first class and had just settled into second period when my teacher noticed that I was not my normal self. I was unusually quiet and settled. At that point, Mrs. Barrett sent me to lie down in the "sick room" for the remainder of the period. As the period ended and students made their way to third period, my third period teacher, Mrs. Blake, showed up in the sick room, wanting to know why I was there. I tried to explain that I was sick, and that Mrs. Barrett had sent me to the room. Nevertheless, Mrs. Blake instructed me to go to her class.

As I sat in class, I felt myself getting weaker, and I was barely able to stay awake. I asked Mrs. Blake if I could go back to the sick room, but I was denied.

In the meanwhile, Mrs. Barrett had apparently gone to the sick room to check on me. When I was gone, she immediately went to the principal's office and reported my apparent illness.

Soon, a call came through the intercom into the Mrs. Blake's classroom.

"Mrs. Blake?" called the principal.

"Yes ... quiet, class, I can't hear!" answered Mrs. Blake. "Yes, Mr. Nutter, may I help you?"

"Do you have James Means in your class right now?"

"Yes, I do."

"Would you please excuse him and bring him to the office immediately?"

"Why certainly, Mr. Nutter. We'll be right down."

I remember that conversation as though it were today. I had not been able to figure out why Mrs. Blake was keeping me in that class when it was more than apparent that I was quite ill. But then again, this *was* Mrs. Blake—the same teacher who would cover that little pane of glass in the center of the door because she believed that people were peeping in at her.

She also took great delight in making the entire class run to the windows when a siren would career by on the street below, and she was always applying the reading textbook to the backside of my best friend, Tim. Since she didn't own a paddle, she used the reading textbook, flailing it about with both hands as she tried to make contact with Tim's backside.

Tim burst out in laughter in the midst the odd spanking, and the class joined in on the laughter. Mrs. Blake's threat to give us the same thing if we didn't hush only added to our laughter.

We made our way down to the school office, and she tried to explain to me why she hadn't excused me in the first place. A call had already been made to Mrs. Means, informing her of my situation. She was already on her way to the school. My afternoon was spent in a makeshift bed upstairs next to the French doors leading out to the sundeck. Fearing I might have a virus, Mrs. Means did not want me in the same room with Steve, lest I spread germs to him.

By that time, I was running a temperature of 102 degrees. That night, I slept very little, dozing off and on. I managed to sleep, but I was awakened by the sensation of becoming sick to my stomach. I won't share the gory details. (You probably know more than you wanted anyway.)

The next day was no better, and I spent the entire day in my makeshift bed. During the early hours of Wednesday morning, I was awakened by a tremendous pain in my abdominal area. As the pain grew, I guessed it must be a tremendous gas pain and thought it would eventually subside. I was right. It did subside after a while. As the pain seemed to peak and began to go away, I felt something inside that I had *never* felt before. It felt like something oozing throughout the inside of my abdominal area.

The next morning, Mrs. Means came upstairs and took my temperature. It was 103 degrees. Without saying a word, she hurried downstairs. I heard her talking on the phone with a doctor's office.

Later that morning, I was taken to a doctor's office in Barboursville, and I was given a light checkup to determine my problem. As I lay on the examining table, the doctor pushed and probed, asking periodically, "Any pain here? Does it hurt when I push in there?" At that point, his pushing and probing *didn't* hurt. His diagnosis simply stated that I was to be admitted into the St. Mary's Hospital in Huntington for "possible appendicitis."

Arriving at the emergency room entrance of St. Mary's Hospital that afternoon, we were met by an elderly nurse with a wheelchair. "Plop yerself right down here, sonny!" she ordered.

I did and was wheeled to another examining table. Being transferred from the chair to the table, I was given another light examination, but this time, it meant getting a blood sample. About two and a half hours later, my white blood cell count came back. It was not good. I was immediately taken to a pediatric ward to await pre-op prep for surgery.

This was a brand-new experience for me. About thirty minutes after arriving to the pediatric ward, I was wheeled into an operating room. As I lay on the operating table, another needle was inserted, which I was told would make me drowsy. They *did not* know me. It was going take a little more than that to put *me* under. And, sure enough, I was still awake when the surgeon came in. I watched as they prepared to do the surgery, and I was still awake when they began to apply the anesthesia. My eyes closed.

I opened my eyes immediately—or so I thought—but a little more than two hours had actually passed. When I began to awaken, I was barely able to open my eyes. My eye lids felt so heavy, and I could barely swallow. I was in my pediatric ward bed surrounded by people. I couldn't figure out who they were at first, but I then heard a very familiar voice saying, "He is so precious!"

Mrs. Manley! Why is she here?

Mrs. Means' voice eventually came through above the others.

As I became more alert to my surroundings, I realized I had a tube passing through my nose and down my throat. That explained the difficulty in swallowing. I looked down to my right side and discovered another tube protruding from my side to a bag attached to the side of the bed. Let's not bother to describe that. Use your own imagination.

A doctor and nurse came to my bedside and pulled back the sheet to reveal a large bandage on the right side of my abdomen. Upon removal of the bandage, I saw a two-to-three-inch wound sewn up with black stitches. It was then that I discovered *another* tube protruding from my side, which was approximately two inches long with a safety pin passing through it. This tube looked something like the open end of a latex balloon sticking out from my side. As gross as it sounds, I soon learned that it was also a drainage tube. Whereas the nasal tube was to drain the poison from my stomach, the balloon-like tube was for the purpose of draining the poison, which had spread throughout my abdomen when my appendix had ruptured that Tuesday night. So *that* was the pain and spreading sensation I had felt!

The next day, I did feel better until the doctor and nurse came by to see how I was getting along. I had been doing well until the doctor began working with my wound. He started by pulling on that balloon tube. That was *not* fun. It felt like he was pulling my insides out, and it seemed like he would never stop. At last, he did, and then he explained that the tube had to be pulled out a little each day so that the tissue would not begin to grow to the tube. That *did* make sense, but it *still* hurt.

The doctor went on to explain to Mrs. Means that my case had been *very* serious. The appendix had ruptured, and the poison had spread so severely throughout my body that it had gotten into my bloodstream. He added that if I had not gotten to the operating room when I did, I would have likely died.

Over the next week, my recovery went well. When I was allowed to go home to recuperate, I was moved to a downstairs bedroom and treated like royalty. I loved it. Kids from my homeroom at school came by one afternoon to visit and brought a copy of the school annual as a gift. That visit meant so much to me because I didn't really realize how much a part of that class I had become.

I seemed to be recuperating quite well for two or three days under the watchful care of Mrs. Means. She played nurse to me, changing the bandage and giving me medicine, but something went wrong. Mrs. Means took my temperature on the third morning, and it had shot back up to 103 degrees. An infection had set in.

I was immediately taken back to the hospital and greeted by the pediatric staff.

"You weren't gone long enough for your bed to get cold. Welcome back!" they said.

I was placed in a different room, and they watched me very closely. After having some tubes reinserted, I began to feel worse. I didn't sleep much that first night, and the nurses were coming and going to give me medicine, take my temperature, and check the bandage.

That pesky balloon tube had been removed and the stitches taken out before I left the hospital the first time. However, the second morning of my reentry to the hospital, I awoke with my side hurting terribly. The nurse came in, and upon removing the bandage, she discovered my initial surgical wound had opened—and some internal tissue was protruding from it. It was decided not to restitch the wound and to keep the tissue submerged inside it. I thought pulling the tube *out* was painful, but each time they pushed the tissue inside, it was a whole new adventure in pain.

Within the next two or three weeks, the wound did begin to heal. I was getting better and was allowed to return home with the hopes that I would be able to return to school. I will end this portion of my story on a much lighter note.

At the end of May, the doctor determined that I was well enough to walk up and down the stairs. I returned to school, having missed most of the six-week term. I was concerned about whether I would pass the seventh grade, but I think Mrs. Blake summed up the situation quite well. Upon returning to her class, she said, "James, I won't penalize you for missing so much class time. I will average your grades according to where you were when you left."

And welcome back to you too, Mrs. Blake! She certainly hadn't gotten better from her illness.

Mrs. Blake did eventually have a nervous breakdown at another school and was "let go." I did pass the seventh grade with the grades I had earned up to the time of my illness, and I was ready to face the challenges of the eighth grade—or so I thought!

Chapter 8

On the Move Again

The school year was finally over, and I was ready for a relaxing, fun-filled summer. Little did I know that another big change was about to take place for Steve and me. Several weeks later, Mr. and Mrs. Means sat down with us and informed us that we would be leaving their home. This came as quite a shock to me because, as far as I knew, there weren't any problems with our living in their home. We were told that we were being moved to a home for children (at that time referred to as an orphanage) called Davis-Stuart School for Children. To make matters worse, we were being moved to the other side of the state in Greenbrier County, West Virginia.

A few days later, Steve and I were taken to Mrs. Manley's office to be given more details about the move. Feeling apprehensive and quite taken unaware with this change, we asked *why* the move was taking place. We were told that the problem was not so much with us as it was with Lou Anne Means. There had been an ongoing conflict between Lou Anne and Steve throughout our stay in the home. Apparently, Mrs. Means had been experiencing some health problems, making it quite difficult to deal with the day-to-day issues between Lou Anne and Steve.

Years later, I learned that the Means had requested to adopt me—but not Steve. The Welfare Department would not agree to that arrangement, maintaining that it would be best for us to remain together.

Then came, yet another, unexpected issue. Think about *this* question: If you were given the opportunity to pick a new last name, what would you choose? That is exactly what we were confronted with. Mrs. Manley asked us how we felt about having *Ying* as our name. Steve and I agreed that we really did not like that name. She said that we could change our last name if we wanted to before moving to the orphanage.

Then came the big question: What would you boys like your last name to be?

Wow! Suddenly, we were faced with a decision that would stay with us for the rest of our lives. Both of us thought hard but could not come up with a name. How do you pick a last name out of thin air?

Then, Mrs. Manley suggested: "How would you boys like to have your mother's maiden name?"

Years earlier, when I had asked Mom Alcie about our real parents, and she had told me that she didn't know much of anything except that our mother's name was Justine Olivia Diehl. That was her maiden name before marrying Jack Ying, whose name appeared on our birth certificates. This suggestion sounded good to both of us, and we settled on our new last name: Diehl.

Plans were made, and the date was set for Steve and me to be relocated to Lewisburg, West Virginia. On the day of the move, we were taken back to the county courthouse to meet our new social worker named. Mr. Wright was from Greenbrier County and would become our new social worker. I think one of the most difficult adjustments was knowing that we would no longer be able to call on Mrs. Manley if we had a problem. At that point, I realized how much I had come to depend on her as a kind of safety net and security blanket. I really hated to say goodbye. Mr. Wright was certainly nice enough, but, given the lifelong relationship we had with Mrs. Manley, it would never be the same.

After saying goodbye to Mrs. Manley, Mr. Wright, Steve, and I loaded up in his car and made our way to Lewisburg. It seemed like we would never get there, but we eventually arrived at our new home: Davis-Stuart School for Children.

CHAPTER 9

BEING INSTITUTIONALIZED AIN'T SO BAD

As we pulled into the drive, a large three-story brick building seemed to loom over us. The administration building housed the staff offices, classrooms, a residential apartment, and a dining hall and kitchen. Staring at that huge building, I became more apprehensive—if not overwhelmed—about the move. There was nothing welcoming about that place.

We were escorted into the administration building, and we met Mrs. Edith Stover. The assistant executive director of the orphanage seemed nice enough, but I didn't feel very comfortable being around her. I was afraid I might do or say something wrong. Not long after that initial meeting, Mr. Wright drove away.

We had arrived just in time to join the other children for lunch in the dining hall. Do you know how it feels when you sense that you are being stared at? That uneasiness was all over me as we waited with the other kids to enter the dining hall. After the meal, we were taken to the houses, or "cottages," as they were called, where we would be living.

Then, another surprise was dropped on me. For the first time in our lives, Steve and I were going to be separated. I would be living at one end of the campus, and he would be living on the other. I was placed in a cottage with about eight or nine other boys, ranging from eight to seventeen years old.

Allow me to add a side note concerning Steve. During the first four years at Davis-Stuart, we rarely spent any time together, and we developed relationships with the other boys in our individual cottages. Steve's interests were more along electronic lines, and mine were more in tune—pardon the pun—with musical performance. We were permanently separated, however, when Steve graduated from high school in 1967 and relocated back to Huntington. Shortly after returning to Huntington, he enlisted in the navy, starting a twenty-seven-year career.

At Davis-Stuart, "house parents" oversaw each cottage. Mr. and Mrs. Williams, an elderly couple, were the house parents for the boys in Davidson Cottage where I was to live. They were like having your grandparents as parents. Mrs. Williams wore a hearing aid that worked—maybe—half the time. The boys often took advantage of that handicap. Mr. Williams was a nice, but very stern man who had no problem handling disciplinary matters with even the oldest teen under his care.

During my first few days in this new environment, it became very apparent that I would have to get established quickly; otherwise, my life was going to be quite miserable. It was, apparently, a common practice for the guys to rummage through the new kid's things during the first few days after arrival, and I was no exception. As I began organizing my belongings, I was surrounded by two or three boys. They were anxious to see what I had. I really didn't mind if they kept their hands off.

Davis-Stuart Home for Children was set on about three hundred acres of cornfields, hayfields, and lots of pastureland. There was also a large dairy of about one hundred Holstein cattle and about fifty beef cattle. These, of course, provided for the milk and beef products needed for the children's home.

To maintain this large farm, the boys—thirteen years and up—were assigned to one of three work crews: the dairy crew, the farm crew, or the garden crew. After a few weeks, I was placed on the dairy crew, which I thought to be a pretty good choice since I had grown up around cattle and considered myself something of an experienced "cowhand." After all, we had milk cows on the farm at Salt Rock that we milked every afternoon by hand. I had also gained experience with horses while looking after Luanne's two horses and one burro. *How much more experience does one need?*

My first afternoon at the dairy barn helped me to realize that no matter how much experience we might think we have in a given area, there is *always* something to be learned. The dairy manager, Mr. Roy Lemons, was a tall, weather-worn man with long, almost orangutan-like arms and the largest hands I had ever seen. Yet, in all his largeness, he was a gentle-spirited man with a great sense of humor.

I had been on the job about five minutes when Lemons—we always called him by his last name—handed me a bucket of soapy water and a sponge and said, "Wash down the cows."

That was something new. In all my experience of milking cows on the farm at Salt Rock, I had *never* been asked to "wash down a cow." However, as Lou Anne's groom for her horses, it was common to wash them down just before a horse show and rub them down at the end of each workout. So, drawing upon my vast experience of animal husbandry, taking my bucket of soapy water and sponge in hand, I began to wash down one of the cows. I figured working from the top down was the best approach.

"What are you doing?" Lemons yelled.

"Washing down the cows like you asked me to," I said, somewhat shocked at his outburst.

"Their udders—wash down their udders! They don't need a whole bath!"

Life at Davis-Stuart School was radically different from living in private foster homes. While each of those private home-life experiences were unique unto themselves, the common thread running through all of them was the "normalcy" of family life. Making the adjustment to the "institutional life" at Davis-Stuart took quite a while. The larger group structure and stricter schedule of everyday life, such as specific mealtimes, strict bed and wake-up times, and work group assignments, meant a strict regimen to which I had never been accustomed.

That being said, one positive affect of having been moved from foster home to foster home was the necessity of becoming flexible to varying life circumstances. This flexibility worked in my favor over the first several months at Davis-Stuart, and I made the adjustment quite well. There were some pluses to this institutional life—not the least of which was learning to accept greater responsibilities and developing better social skills as I related to the other kids at Davis-Stuart.

Within the first two years of living there, Davis-Stuart underwent several changes that had definite effects on the residents. For example, the cottages were transformed from being single-gender-only cottages to being co-ed cottages. This change, alone, created some interesting, if not questionable, issues for the house parents and residents. As we adjusted to this change, some of the expected issues arose when boys and girls coexist under the same roof. It became more of a "brother-sister relationship," and common sibling rivalries soon surfaced, resulting in arguments and even just good old-fashioned fights.

Living within the realm of institutional life, the Davis-Stuart campus became my world. Everything I did was limited to the campus. We went to school on campus, the entire social structure was limited to campus life, and we attended church in the campus chapel. The executive director of Davis-Stuart was Mr. Robert Hawks. At the time of my arrival on campus, Mr. Hawks had been the director for a relatively short time. As with any administrative change, Mr. Hawks brought new ideas and various infrastructural changes to Davis-Stuart.

Many of these changes made were considered by some—especially the board of directors, as I learned years later—too radically different from the previous executive director. Shifting away from separate cottages for boys and girls to co-ed cottages was just one of those questionable changes. Under Mr. Hawks' leadership, the junior high and high school students no longer were confined to the classrooms on campus, and they were enrolled in a local public school.

During the first semester in the public school, the Davis-Stuart kids were often ridiculed by other students. Some said, "Here come the little orphans!" That did not sit well with any of us. While we might have fought like siblings on campus, it did not take long for the harassing students to discover that, if they took on one Davis-Stuart kid, they had to take on the lot of us. We stood our ground united.

Perhaps the most significant change was that we would no longer worship in the campus chapel. Since Davis-Stuart was sponsored by the Presbyterian Church, we began attending the Ronceverte Presbyterian Church. This change had its own set of problems; the least of which was transporting the kids and staff to the church. New vans were purchased to alleviate this problem.

Then, there was the issue of making room in the downtown church Sunday school classes to accommodate the "Davis-Stuart invasion." Classes that had been averaging four or five students now had as many as seven to ten additional students for which to plan and prepare. As it eventually turned out, the junior high and high school students of Davis-Stuart became the youth department, and only four or five local kids participated in the youth program.

I became active in the church music program, and I sang in both the youth and (eventually) adult choirs. I also became involved in the youth program, and I eventually served as an officer on the Greenbrier Presbytery District 3 Youth Council. This early youth ministry gave me an opportunity to participate in summer youth camp and participate in church services in other communities as a guest worship leader.

CHAPTER 10

MUSIC: GOD'S GIFT FOR A TROUBLED SOUL

Martin Luther wrote, "Music is one of the fairest and most glorious gifts of God, to which Satan is a bitter enemy, for it removes from the heart the weight of sorrow, and the fascination of evil thoughts."

Everyone needs to have a medium for venting the suppressed emotions that result from any form of crisis or trauma. One definition of "crisis" I learned in seminary was "any event that causes extreme change in one's life—be it positive or negative." For some people, the emotions resulting from such crises may surface negatively through anger and actions thereof. For others, suppressed emotions can be expressed through positive avenues such as various art forms. Although I have never openly expressed or acknowledged any emotional consequences from all the changes I experienced throughout childhood and adolescence, I must honestly say that, at times, I feel the internal urge to let go of my emotions.

God has directed me, like so many others, through those crises times as well. From an early age, I loved music and found various means of expressing myself through music. I had learned how to play the guitar during the year before moving to Davis-Stuart. During eighth grade, I decided to become a school band member—with the notion of learning how to play the drums. Since beginning band class was primarily for seventh graders, I was the oldest student in the class. That first day in class was both an exciting one and a letdown. Allow me to explain.

One of the first activities of that class was to select which instrument we wanted to learn how to play. In those days, not many students owned their own instruments, and they were largely dependent on instruments available through the school.

Our band director, Mrs. Legg, went around the room and asked each student what instrument they wanted to play. When she came to me, I was ready. There was no question, nor any hesitancy. "I wanna play the drums!"

"Well, we only have a few drums, and they're all taken now," she replied.

Now what? I have no idea what else to pick.

"Is there any other instrument you might like to try?"

Then, it hit me. I remembered a guy in the sixth grade who played an instrument called a saxophone. So, with big smile on my face, I blurted out, "A saxophone!"

She said, "Which one?"

That one got me! I didn't care—any old saxophone was fine with me.

Seeing my confused look, she said, "Would you want to play the tenor sax or the alto sax?"

Since I didn't know one from the other, she suggested that I begin on the tenor since that was the most available instrument. It was with that decision, made totally under the circumstance and out of pure ignorance, that I began my musical career as a sax player.

Beginners' band went quite well, and at the beginning of ninth grade, I advanced to the high school band. As my proficiency developed on the sax, Mrs. Legg wanted me to add another instrument to my skills. As it happened, since the band became in need of a bell lyre player, I was given that assignment. With the guidance of Mrs. Legg, I mastered the lyre, which was simply a vertical xylophone, and I spent the winter concert season in the percussion section.

Between my junior and senior year, a new consolidated high school was opened, which created the necessity to transfer to Greenbrier East High School. While Mrs. Legg had been an excellent instructor, transferring to the Greenbrier East High would open new and greater opportunities to grow and develop in my music.

During my senior year, under the direction of Lee Gillespie, I had opportunities to play in small orchestras for extracurricular events, including the summer stock community theater. In addition to playing the sax, I became active in the school choral music program, eventually having opportunities to perform in all-county choruses and an audition choral ensemble.

I also began giving some serious thought to pursuing a career as a high school music director.

As with most every other teenager, I loved the sound of rock 'and roll music. During the mid to late sixties, small rock groups, "combos," were popping up all over the place, and our area was no different. The Davis-Stuart administrative staff recognized this and allowed me, along with two other on-campus guys and one guy who lived in Lewisburg, to form our own combo. "The Shades of Knight," our four-man rock group, consisted of lead and bass guitarists, a drummer, and a lead singer. A large part of the fun was that we actually played for high school dances and some private dance bookings. As we developed our rock skills and added a second guitar and keyboard, we became as well-known as other local combos and were invited to compete in local battles of the bands. We never won first place, but, two or three times, we did manage to pull out a second place.

Music was not my only interest during those teen years. Although I was never a good athlete, I decided to try out for the high school track team. I specialized in the 440-yard dash and the mile relay. During those two years of track and field, I discovered a great truth to remember: There is no shame in finishing dead last. Someone always will.

CHAPTER 11

FROM ROCK BOTTOM TO THE TOP OF THE MOUNTAIN

Upon graduating from high school in May 1969, I left Davis-Stuart and returning to the Means' home in Huntington, West Virginia. The plan was to enroll at Marshall University for the fall semester. My departure from Davis-Stuart was very abrupt. Leaving that same night of graduation, I did not have enough time to say goodbye to those with whom I had spent the past five years.

The summer of 1969 meant another big adjustment: moving from institutional life and returning to a private home setting. Although moving back into the Means home, I was not prepared for the readjustment to private life. I was no longer living under a strict regimen, and my time was pretty much my own. For the most part, I had no clue what to do with myself. In hopes of earning money for my first semester at Marshall University, I got a job working in an automobile bumper factory and later as a "curb hop" for a couple of local restaurants.

In September 1969, I began my freshman year at Marshall University as a music education major, once again, finding myself to be woefully unprepared. It did not take very long to figure that out. I was not "making the grade," so to speak. I won't bore you with details of my downward spiral, except to say that I went off the proverbial deep end, getting involved in drugs and alcohol.

This lifestyle continued as my grade point average plunged to the point of being placed on academic probation. Finally, by May of 1971, I had had enough. In my frustration, I decided that I did not need that aggravation. With the use of uppers, alcohol, and a constant usage of No-Doz, I was wired. For the most part, I was unable to maintain any focus on anything. I dropped out of school and continued my self-destructive lifestyle.

By June of 1971, I had become a night owl, spending most nights in my car, parked on an abandoned boat ramp along the Ohio River. After going nonstop for days at a time and getting very little sleep, the physical effects of my lifestyle finally took their toll on me. One evening while at work, I crashed. I felt like my entire body was shutting down, I was barely able to sit upright—let alone stand. A tremendous feeling of anxiety and uncontrollable emotion took over my body. I felt like I was going to explode and could do nothing to prevent it. At that point, I did not care if I lived or died. I felt like my life had finally reached the bottom.

I was told to clock out and go home if I couldn't work. From that point, I have no remembrance of where I went or how I got there. Days later, I came to the realization that if I continued down that path, I would surely die. During that time, God did something totally unexpected. He had allowed me to go my own self-destructive way until I came to the realization that I needed something beyond myself to pull me out of the mire into which I had fallen.

With that realization and some intentional changes in my daily lifestyle, I was able to function more rationally—and I even began to feel better. During that time, a close friend of mine and his fiancé, with whom I had shared an apartment, decided to get married. Although I was dead set against anyone getting married, I agreed to serve as his best man. Later that evening, having stopped at a drive-in restaurant, the curb hop came to get my order. Always on the lookout for an attractive girl, I began flirting with the waitress. She didn't say too much other than getting my food order and going back inside the restaurant.

In a few minutes, a different girl returned with my food. Apparently, the first waitress didn't think too highly of me. That was quite okay though because this one was even cuter, and I wanted to get to know her. There was something very different about her from any girl I had ever met. As strange as it might seem, the first waitress was the twin sister of the second. We struck up a brief conversation, concluding that anyone who got married was pretty much out of their mind (each of us for our own different reasons).

We began seeing each other on short, casual outings in the city park and talking on the phone. She and her family lived in a small mobile home park, and I would go by to pick her up for a date. Her parents were usually at work, and I never saw them.

This relationship continued on a casual basis for a few weeks, and she never mentioned anything about meeting her parents. At the time, I didn't know anything about her parents—other than they had recently moved to the Huntington area from Kentucky. Then, it happened.

On our way to an outing, she suddenly exclaimed, "There goes my dad! Wanna meet him?"

I immediately turned the car around and followed his car to their home.

It really wasn't so much what she had told me about her parents. It was more of what she *had not* told me about them, especially her dad. While we were driving back to her house, she revealed that her dad was a Baptist preacher. Glaring at her, I asked her to repeat that. The one thing I did not want to get caught up in was dating the daughter of a preacher. That went totally against my way of life. Most likely, had I known that when we first met, I would have broken off the relationship.

However, it was too late for that. I had become very fond of her and wanted to continue being with her. We pulled in behind her dad's car just in time to see him getting out and walking toward the front door. What I saw was a complete shock and totally unexpected. Standing just a few yards in front of me was a tall, slender man sporting a sharp blazer, a Samsonite attaché case, and a longer-style haircut that was not typical of most men his age—let alone a preacher!

"That's your dad?" I asked in amazement.

She acknowledged that he was and that it was time to meet both of her parents.

Being totally out of my comfort zone, I didn't know how to act or what to say. That was okay since her parents sensed my uneasiness and began the conversation. They were very kind and made me feel more at ease. I learned that her dad was the manager of a new radio station in Huntington—a Christian radio station. This got my attention. I had always had the notion of being a "disc jockey," but Christian radio?

As our relationship continued, our conversations became more personal. Then, one night, it became *very* personal.

"Jim," she asked, "are you a Christian?"

Whoa—where did that come from? I thought for a moment and said, "I think so."

She said, "You have to know for sure," and she left it at that.

A few months later, Bob Harrington, the "chaplain of Bourbon Street" was holding an evangelistic crusade in Huntington. I was invited to go on Monday night with my girlfriend's family. I told them I would meet them there, but I didn't show up.

When I called her the next day, she said, "Where were you?"

It was no use trying to make excuses, and I agreed that I would be there on Wednesday night.

She replied firmly, "Look, if you don't wanna go, that's fine. Just don't tell me that you'll be there and not show up."

I felt like a real jerk. It was decided that I would pick her up, and we would go together.

That was the best decision I had ever made. That night, God showed me that—in spite of turning my back on Him— He never turned His back on me. That night, Bob Harrington preached about "the four biggest fools in Huntington, West Virginia." I realized that I was one of those "fools." When the appeal was given for people to give their hearts to Jesus for salvation, I held onto the chair in front of me as though for dear life.

After two stanzas of the song, Harrington stopped the singing, stating that it could be the last time some of us would have an opportunity to receive Christ. In that moment, it was as though he was speaking directly to me. At the same time, I remembered a decision I had made years ago at the Pea Ridge Baptist Church—but I also knew what my life had been like until recently.

Without saying a word, or even looking at my girlfriend, I let go and made my way to speak with a counselor. For the first time, I heard the "plan of salvation." That was the night in August 1971 when I surrendered my life to Christ. Those of us responding to the appeal were escorted to another counseling area behind the stage to be counseled further about our decision. Being caught up in the moment, I realized that I had totally forgotten about my girlfriend. When I looked up and saw her walking toward me in the hallway, I said, "Now, I know for sure!"

My girlfriend's dad was the station manager of WEMM-FM. In our conversations, I had mentioned that I had always had an interest in being a disc jockey. Having become more acquainted with me, and knowing of my decision to become a Christian, her dad presented a challenge to me. For a person to be on the air in broadcasting, an FCC license was required, and it could only be obtained by passing a written exam. If I would study, take, and pass the exam, I would be put on the air at WEMM.

After several weeks of intense study, I went to Detroit, Michigan, with his son to take the exam. I was completely surprised when I passed the exam! Living up to his promise, my girlfriend's dad put me on the air from Monday through Friday at midnight to five o'clock in the morning!

CHAPTER 12

YOU'RE IN THE ARMY NOW!

The rest of August and September were delightful, and I enjoyed my newfound freedom to live decently and in good order. I was baptized and joined the Westmoreland Baptist Church, where my girlfriend's family attended, and her dad was filling in for the pastor who was ill. Along with attending on Sunday mornings, I began attending some youth functions at the church. Continuing my work at the restaurant, I also continued working the midnight shift at WEMM-FM. My girlfriend and I would spend time playing in the city park and going out on dates. Finally, life was good!

Then, it arrived! "Greetings from Your Uncle Sam!" Yep, I was drafted and ordered to report to the local Armed Forces Entrance Examination Station (AFEES).

Just when things are going great, this happened!

Remember the regimented life at Davis-Stuart of which I spoke earlier? Well, it was back to that regimented life. I didn't mind; I had been there. On November 11, 1971, I became Private James Diehl, USA. Having recently enlisted into the Lord's Army, I was now ready for His service. I had been baptized and joined the Westmoreland Baptist Church, and I was eager to serve the Lord wherever He wanted—but in the army?

As usual, God had this all worked out. During my first days at Fort Knox, Kentucky, for basic training, I learned of the chaplaincy program through which a soldier could serve as a chaplain's assistant. There it was! The writing was on the wall, and I read every word. I applied for the training, and I waited. Many weeks later, at the close of my basic training, I received my orders. At last—I was gonna serve the Lord as a chaplain's assistant. Wrong!

I had received orders for Clerk School where I would train to be a company clerk. That was *not* in my plans—or God's, I surmised. I went, of course, and at the conclusion of my Advanced Individual Training (AIT) program, I found myself awaiting orders again. Then, I got the call. I was to report to the Reception Station Chapel for on-the-job training (OJT) with Chaplain Major Merrill Challman.

God had done it again. He knew I needed the office training to carry out my duties as a chaplain's assistant. I was ready to move forward in ministry under the guidance of a godly man whose primary concern was ministering to soldiers' needs. The next three to four months were a great learning and growing experience. I was serving the Lord while serving in the US Army.

One afternoon, my office phone rang.

"Triangle Chapel, Private Diehl speaking."

It was from the Post Chaplain's Office. "Hey, Diehl, pack your duffel bag. You're shipping out!"

Shipping out? To where? When? And more importantly, why?

As it turned out, another chaplain's assistant and I had been selected to be transferred for temporary duty (TDY) in Bowling Green, Virginia, as ration breakdown clerks. This was totally off my radar. I obeyed, of course, and I spent the summer of 1972 in the hot, humid, and muggy Camp A. P. Hill.

I kept thinking, "*Why is God sending me there?*"

As it happened, a church in downtown Bowling Green needed a summer music director. While working charge of quarters (CQ) one night, I received a call. The person on the other end of the line asked to speak with a James Diehl.

"That's me!"

He shared their need and explained that he understood I had studied music. He wanted to know if I would be available and willing to lead their worship music for the summer. I was completely surprised and wondered how he knew about my music background. Nevertheless, I accepted his offer and spent the summer of 1972 directing the music at the Caroline Baptist Church in Bowling Green, Virginia.

I remained at the "Hill" until the middle of September, and then I was ordered back to Fort Knox to continue my service as a chaplain's assistant. Shortly after returning to my duties with Chaplain Challman, he announced his retirement. A new chaplain was brought in, but our relationship was less than favorable. I transferred to another chapel. At the 194th Armor Brigade Chapel, I served double duty as the chaplain's assistant and choral director for another chapel. God's plan was slowly being revealed. I had just spent four months in choral music ministry at the Caroline Baptist Church in Bowling Green, Virginia.

Having attained my permanent party status back at Fort Knox, my work hours were basically an eight-to-five workday, Monday through Friday. Although I had to work every Sunday, I did have Saturdays off. Occasionally, I would go to a little town just a few miles off post to relax among civilians. During one of those trips, I dropped by a local radio station to speak with the manager and, perhaps, get a tour of their facilities. My FCC license was still active, and I wanted to explore the possibility of getting hired on a part-time basis.

As long as a civilian employment did not interfere or conflict with my military duties, there was not a problem with the army. I was given a "radio check audition" by the manager and was hired as a weekend newscaster at WROC-AM.

By now, you may be asking yourself, "Who is this girlfriend he keeps talking about—and what happened to that relationship?" She and I managed to continue our relationship, albeit a long-distance one. During that first year of army life, I went back and forth to see her and her family on many occasions. During that same period, she and her parents would travel to Fort Knox to visit with me and tour the post.

February 3, 1973 is a date second only to that August night in 1971 when I became a Christian. On a cold and rainy night, Karen Klingler, the daughter of Rev. and Mrs. Ken Klingler, and I were married at the Highlawn Baptist Church in Huntington, West Virginia. I should also mention that I was honored to have Mom Alcie and Poppy Scott DeJarnett stand in for me as "parents of the groom." I had considered them—and still do—to be the closest parental relationship I had ever experienced.

Karen was that special instrument in God's hand who made me realize that my life needed to change. I realized the only way for that to happen was for me to surrender my life to Christ Jesus. Karen was an instrument of God and encouraged me as He matured me, giving me opportunities to serve Him more effectively.

Kar and I made our first home together in Valley Station, Kentucky, not far off-post, near Louisville, Kentucky. Leaving civilian life to be a military wife meant that Kar had some adjustments to make in addition to getting used to married life. Living on a modest budget, we had to find inexpensive outside fun opportunities. We discovered that we could go to the airport in Louisville and play "Pong," a video tennis game quite inexpensively. I know it sounds terribly boring, but for us, it was loads of fun—and it was cheap entertainment.

Every so often, Karen would go with me on post, and she soon became a familiar face among some of my fellow chaplain's assistants, including Bill and Forrest. Forrest and I were very good friends, and we had spent a lot of time hanging out before I married Karen. When Karen came, all three of us would hang out together. Some of those hangout times included playing practical tricks on Karen. For example, as you are likely aware, Fort Knox is the home of the US Gold Depository. You may have seen pictures or postcards showing the depository, looking up a long driveway. At night, however, the depository is lit up and is truly a beautiful sight. I always enjoyed driving by and looking at it, and I thought Karen would enjoy it as well.

What the average person does not see in those publicity pictures of the depository are the large signs warning would-be intruders not to go any farther into the driveway. These—added to the large speakers giving a verbal warning—can be intimidating, if not frightening, to unsuspecting people. With that in mind, I decided that Forrest and I should treat Karen to this wonderful sight of the depository. I did not happen to mention the warnings. With all three of us in the front seat, I drove down Bullion Boulevard—straight to the depository entrance.

I managed to drive just far enough into the driveway entrance to set off the warning alarms. With huge lights shining on us and loud verbal warnings telling us we had exceeded the boundary—and must vacate the premises immediately—we left the area with one very shaken lady in the car. Somehow, she did not find that trick as humorous as Forrest and I did. We played other practical tricks on Kar over the next few weeks, but she soon became accustomed to the military way of life—and the practical tricks were no longer effective.

Nine months later—on November 10, 1973—I was released from active duty. I had to decide what to do and where to do it. Our choices were limited. Karen's family had moved from West Virginia to Deland, Florida. Since it was nearly winter—and since I had no "real" family in West Virginia or imminent plans for employment—Karen and I made the only sensible decision, which was to relocate to Florida. She would be near her family, and it was definitely warmer than being in West Virginia in November.

After getting reasonably settled in Florida, I went to managerial school for the McDonald's Corporation, eventually working in a McDonald's restaurant as a shift manager.

CHAPTER 13

THE CALL NEVER EXPECTED

Shortly after arriving in Florida, I received managerial training for McDonald's and became a shift manager at a unit in Eustis, Florida, north of Orlando. Since I was the evening manager, I was able to get additional work at WLCO, a local AM radio station as the midmorning announcer. Meanwhile, less than desirable circumstances at McDonald's led me to apply for another job as a dispatcher for the Volusia County Sheriff's Department, and I remained there through December 1974.

During this period, I sensed God calling me into ministry as a minister of music. In January 1975, God called me to serve the Westside Baptist Church as minister of music and youth. Wanting to continue my education, I enrolled at Daytona Beach Community College to recover from the poor academic standing I had left at Marshall University. I completed the two-year program and received an associate degree in music. This accomplishment enabled me to enroll into Stetson University in Deland, Florida, as a music education major.

After finishing at Stetson University, I was called to Fort Lauderdale as minister of music and youth. I served there until I received a call from the Central Baptist Church in Melbourne, Florida, and then I served as their minister of music and youth. After having served at Central Baptist four years, I was called to serve a new church under the umbrella of the Melbourne First Baptist Church. While there, I was called by that church to work as the full-time morning announcer at WCIF-FM, a Christian radio station. I had returned to the radio format with which I began in 1971.

During all those years, I had given very little thought concerning my early childhood years. It was not until around 1981 that the answers began to fall into place. One evening, the phone rang.

Karen answered, giving me the impression—from her voice—that it was my brother.

I had not heard from Steve in many years.

She said, "Some man is asking for 'Jimmy.'"

No one ever called me *that* except those who knew me as a child.

When I picked up the receiver, a man's voice said, "Is this Jimmy?"

"Yes, it is. May I ask who this is?"

"Jimmy, I believe I am your father."

I was stunned. That was the one call I had never expected to receive. Regaining my focus, I asked why this man thought he was my father.

He told me that his name was Julian Caldwell, and he explained that he and my mother, Justine, had had a relationship in the late forties and early fifties and had relocated to California. This information was not totally news to me since I had been told throughout the years that my mother had, indeed, run off with a taxicab driver named Julian Caldwell and that they had moved to California. In fact, while living in the Martin's foster home, Charlie Martin had told us that he knew of a Julian Caldwell, a taxicab driver in Huntington, West Virginia.

After speaking with Mr. Caldwell, I concluded that if anyone was truly my biological father, it was him. I won't go into the details of that revealing conversation except to relate one portion of it.

After listening to Mr. Caldwell for several minutes, I said, "Sir, I'm glad that you called, but why are you calling me now?"

"Guilt," he said.

"Guilt over what?" I asked.

"Over not having fulfilled my responsibility to both of you boys as your father."

What follows is the most important part of our conversation, verbatim: "Mr. Caldwell, are you a Christian? Have you ever given your life to the Lord?"

"Yes," he answered.

I said, "Have you ever sought His forgiveness?"

"Yes, many times," he answered.

"Well, sir, do you not believe that God has forgiven you for all of that?"

"Oh, yes."

"Well, sir, you have been carrying that guilt around needlessly for many years."

"But, Jimmy, I need your forgiveness."

I was very moved by his confession and said, "Mr. Caldwell … yes, you did drop the ball as our earthly father, but I want you to understand that where you dropped that ball, my heavenly Father picked it up and carried us through all those years. I forgave you a long time ago."

We went on to discuss some other things that are not important for this account. I will never forget that conversation. It was the only time I ever spoke to Julian Caldwell, my earthly father.

During the next several years, God expanded my ministry. He led Karen and me to east Tennessee, and I served as minister of music and youth at the Alpha Baptist Church in Morristown. I had begun to sense God's calling for me to return to school and pursue a biblical studies degree. As usual, God opened that door. Carson-Newman College—now Carson-Newman University—was just ten miles from my church. I enrolled and received my Bachelor of Arts in religion in 1986.

The Lord expanded my ministry, and He also expanded our family with a son. It is truly amazing how the Lord will use a person's background to provide a heart of understanding for the present. Karen and I had been told that we could not have any biological children. Having accepted that as God's will, we sensed His desire for us to consider adoption. While living in Melbourne, Florida, we experienced great heartbreak from an adoption process, which failed due to the biological mother's change of mind after the babies were born. Yes, it was twins.

That experience left both of us very hurt and, perhaps, angry at the Lord for taking us through the entire process over many months—just to have everything taken from us. Much healing of the heart needed to happen for both of us. I firmly believe it was part of the reason the Lord opened the door of ministry in Tennessee, removing us from the area in which we had been devastated. We resigned ourselves to the apparent fact that the Lord did not intend for us to have children.

On a Wednesday morning, while I was sitting in my office at the Alpha Baptist Church, the phone rang. The friend in Florida who had worked with us during the adoption process informed me that another baby would be available for adoption very soon.

I immediately rejected his suggestion, reminding him that we could not and would not open ourselves to another heartbreaking situation.

However, he persisted. He went on to assure me that it would not happen if we would at least give it prayerful consideration. I agreed to discuss it with Karen and told him I would get back with him.

After prayerful consideration of all the reasons why we should *not* go through this again, we could not get past the one reason why we *should*. Why would the Lord open this door, knowing how much hurt we had experienced? He must have a reason. So it was that we agreed to pursue the adoption. Without going step by step through the coming weeks and months, I will tell you that we did, in fact, go through the process —even with one major and unexpected problem.

Several weeks into the process, I received a call from the Department of Human Services in Melbourne, Florida. We were being turned down for the adoption for the simple reason that we lived out of state because all out-of-state adoptions were banned. Not being able to accept this, I insisted that there *must* be a way to carry on the process. The DHS agent insisted there was not. I could not accept this as final and decided to take the matter to the director of the Florida Department of Human Services at the state capital.

After listening to this person, it did not seem like we would be able to adopt the child when he or she would be born. Then, God did it again. The door opened. The director remembered a case that had set a very brief precedence—and thereby a loophole—for an out-of-state adoption to occur. The loophole was only open through the end of April of that year.

"When is the baby due?" she asked.

"The first part of April," I replied. This was the answer I had sought. It meant that we would need to make a couple trips from Tennessee to Florida, but we didn't care.

Kenneth Scott Diehl was given to us on Wednesday, April 4, 1984. We carried him to our home in Tennessee three days later. Having spoken again with the DHS agent in Melbourne, I discovered that the only reason—from their perspective—we were able to complete the adoption was because our file from the previous attempt had not yet been closed. In other words, God allowed us to go through the heartbreaking experience, knowing that He had something special for us two years later. Had we not gone through that, we would not have had an open file. I tell you all of this to show you how the Lord took a baby born in 1951 without a family and led him to the point of also taking a baby boy without a family and giving him one in 1984.

Karen and I had been told that the chances of her conceiving were 99.999 percent against it. Wouldn't you know it? We discovered that Karen was pregnant in 1985, and on April 27, 1986, Bryan Anthony Diehl was given to us. Two miraculous events! I realize all births are true miracles but given the human circumstances surrounding each of our sons' births, they can be explained only as God working His perfect, miraculous will in all our lives.

It was also during my tenure at Alpha Baptist Church that I sensed God leading me into pastoral/preaching ministry. Having graduated from Carson-Newman and having begun work on my master's degree, I accepted the call in September of that year to serve as pastor of the Floyd's Creek Baptist Church in Forest City, North Carolina. During my thirteen-year tenure at Floyd's Creek, I continued my education, receiving both a Master of Arts in biblical studies and a Doctor of Theology degree.

Henry Blackaby, in *Experiencing God*, wrote that as we seek God's will for our lives, God always uses opportunities when and where we are as preparation for what He desires for us in the future. I am a firm believer in that fact. Having ministered for twenty-four years as a staff member and a pastor, I now realize that God was preparing me for another area of ministry to which I had never given any thought.

At the end of those thirteen years as pastor, I received and accepted the call to serve the Lord as the director of missions of the Sandy Run Baptist Association. I served that association for nine years, and then I was called serve as director of the Aiken Baptist Association in Aiken, South Carolina.

CHAPTER 14

AND THE TRUTH SHALL SET YOU FREE

Have you ever been to a movie that began with the time setting in the present, but then it immediately takes you back in time? Call it a flashback if you will. The flashback is designed to give the viewer a backdrop of events leading up to the present time.

Up until now, I have attempted to make you aware of events as they occurred, beginning in January 1956. Unanswered questions loomed over me for many years: Why did certain events transpire as they did? Why were Steve and I removed from the security of a loving home with the DeJarnetts? How did the Welfare Department not know of the abuses taking place at the Martins?

This is the mysterious backdrop with which I began this autobiographical account. It was never any big secret that I was a "foster" child. That was the label I lived with for many years. It was never "This is our son." Rather, it was more on the order of "This is one of the boys we're keeping" or "This is one of our foster children." From the time I went to live with the DeJarnetts, I asked questions: Who is my "real" mother? Where are my "real" parents? I have quite vivid memories of these inquiries, but the only answer I was given was my mother's name: Justine Olivia Diehl. What about our "real" daddy?

According to birth records, a man by the name of Jack Ying was our father. I often asked about that, especially when I realized that the name was Chinese. I certainly didn't look Chinese, although it was often said that my eyes had an Asian appearance in my early years. I was jokingly called the "little Chinaman" when I was five or six years old. That never really bothered me. What did bother me was having to explain to other kids why my last name was so weird; after all, I certainly didn't look Chinese.

When I asked about my "real" mother, Mom Alcie DeJarnett would give me answers about our beginnings, according to what the State Welfare Department had revealed to her. From her account, our mother had left Steve and me with a babysitter—or a friend—expecting to return within a matter of days. She never came back. Who was this person? When had this occurred? Where did my mother go? To the best of my understanding at that time, I was under a year old, and Steve was around two years old, when our mother left. Steve always maintained that he remembered our mother, and he would describe her as "very beautiful with black hair and beautiful skin." He added that he remembered eating oatmeal from pie pans and eating cold hot dogs. Throughout my childhood and teenage years, that was the totality of my understanding about our early years.

Now, fast-forward to the summer of 1969. My longing to understand more about my "real" family intensified during that summer, and I decided to search for answers. Let me recount one such occurrence. In the fall of 1969, I had entered Marshall University. Not having a car of my own, I often walked up and down the streets of Huntington, West Virginia, for lack

of anything to occupy my time. I had known that my alleged
father was the owner/operator of the New China Restaurant
on Third Avenue in Huntington. One day, while walking
along Third Avenue, I happened to walk past the New China
Restaurant. I stopped and wondered whether I should go in. If
I did, what would I say? How do you ask a person if he is your
real father?

I tried out a few approaches to myself, but all of them seemed
lame—even to me. However, my hunger for understanding
overcame my fear of sounding stupid. I slowly entered the
restaurant. It was somewhat dark inside, and I made my way to
a counter off to the left.

A man, seemingly of Asian descent, apparently in his early
to mid-forties, was standing at the far end of the counter.
"Yes ... what you want?" he asked.

At that point, I really didn't have a clue what I should do or
say, but I gave what I considered to be my best shot.

"Is Jack Ying here?"

"Why?"

"I ... want to talk to him," I stuttered, hoping not to sound
as nervous or as frightened as I felt.

"What do you want to talk to him about?" he asked.

I could not believe what came out of my mouth next.
"That's between me and him. I think I might be his son. My
mother is Justine Diehl."

He quickly came from behind the counter toward me,
raising his voice in apparent anger. I, quite honestly, do not
know what that man said. By the time he had made his way to
the front of the counter, I had begun walking toward the front
door, wanting to get out of there as quickly as possible.

Once outside the restaurant, I hurried down the street,
occasionally glancing back to make sure I wasn't being followed

by the entire Chinese community. That had not gone too well, but I had not expected to receive such a hostile response. I thought about that incident from time to time and concluded that I had come face-to-face with Jack Ying.

That encounter fueled my desire to search further and deeper for the truth about my biological family. Having stayed in contact with the DeJarnetts while at Davis-Stuart School, I learned that a new neighbor, a few miles up the road from Mom Alcie and Poppy Scott, had known a man who may have been my real father. This information was solidified while living in the Martin home.

It seems that Charlie Martin was familiar with some of the staff of the Black and White Cab company in Huntington, West Virginia. One morning, he took Steve and me downtown to the cab company, and we were shown an old photograph of some cab drivers. Charlie pointed out a man who he claimed was Julian Caldwell, our biological father, but I didn't know whether to believe him or not. I basically dismissed the idea, but I kept it in the back of my mind for the next several years.

In fact, it was not until 1992 that I began to contemplate this whole background mystery once again. I decided that I needed to put it to rest—once and for all. Thus, began a more intensive search for the truth about my real family. I was able to gather records from the West Virginia Department of Welfare and the *Huntington Herald-Dispatch* newspaper, and I was even able to locate the attorney who had handled Jack Ying's divorce from Justine.

Armed with evidence gathered from those sources, I renewed my search for the truth about my family. Perhaps the most significant discovery I made was that I had a half-sister, Jackie, who was, in fact, the daughter of my mother and Jack Ying. I was able to determine that Jackie—now Jackie Sloan—

was an RN at a hospital near Charleston, West Virginia. I called her, and we set a date for me to meet with her and her husband in Hurricane, West Virginia. What I discovered from her about our mother was extremely valuable in putting together the missing pieces of this puzzle.

The other significant discovery was the name and phone number of the mysterious lady with whom my mother had left Steve and me when she left. Her name was Mrs. Enid Tomblin, and she was still living in Huntington. Upon discovery of her phone number, I called her. The phone rang two or three times—and then the voice of an obviously aged woman answered. "Hello?" It was the voice of the previously mysterious person who seemed to be the so-called missing link for which I had been searching.

The voice repeated, "Hello?"

I said, "Mrs. Tomblin, my name is James Diehl, but you may remember me as Jimmy Ying. My mother was Justine Olivia Diehl."

Her immediate response took me by surprise. With a scream—apparently mixed with tears—she cried out, "Jimmy! I knew that I would hear from you one day!"

It was truly a sweet conversation and a very telling one. Mrs. Tomblin shared the story of how and when my mother had often left her children with her, but she always came back to get them.

Wanting to learn more about those early days, I asked Mrs. Tomblin if she would mind if I came to meet with her and her surviving family. She readily agreed, and the meeting was set. At that visit, I also met her daughter, who remembered me as a baby, and shared stories of how she would hold me on her lap. Then, best of all, they had pictures. *Pictures!* It was a gold mine of information I had never expected to uncover. I asked if I might borrow the pictures to make copies. They hesitantly agreed, not wanting to have them gone from their possession. I assured them that I would return them, and they let them go. During that visit, Mrs. Tomblin and her daughter related the events of the day my mother left Steve and me with her.

According to Mrs. Tomblin, my mother left in February 1951, saying she would return in about two weeks. Although she called Mrs. Tomblin from time to time, Justine never returned for us. It seems that she had told Jackie and her sister, Mary Jean, that she was going to Texas for a while, but would soon return. This story differed from what she had told Mrs. Tomblin. She told the Tomblins that she was going to California for a short while. That was the last time she was seen. Having been rejected by the Yings, Steve and I were taken in by the Tomblins as part of their family where we lived with several children and some elderly people they looked after.

As she had promised, Justine sent a little bit of money for a short time, but she soon stopped sending it. At that point, Mrs. Tomblin called the Department of Welfare in hopes of receiving some financial assistance for keeping us as foster children. This request resulted in a home visit from the Welfare Department, whereupon they discovered that our living conditions were undesirable by their standards. The Welfare Department then took steps to have Steve and me removed from the Tomblin home. I am now ready to lay out the basic facts as I discovered them.

Armed with the information Mrs. Tomblin—also spelled *Tomlin* in some documents—had provided, I contacted a sister-in-law of Justine's in Sylvester, West Virginia. According to her, my mother was a "very unsettled individual who, could never stay in one place and was very flighty." Added to that, she got involved with alcohol, eventually becoming an alcoholic. Due to her lascivious lifestyle, she became known as the black sheep of the family. In fact, according to a report from the West Virginia Department of Welfare, although Justine Ying had told Mrs. Tomlin that her parents were both dead, Mrs. Tomlin learned, during her efforts to locate Mrs. Ying, that her mother was living. [Mrs. Tomlin] wrote to Mrs. Ying's mother, Sally Workman ... Mrs. Workman replied that her husband ... had died a few years ago. She [Sally] had remarried and had a house-full, herself, so, couldn't take the children. She expressed displeasure with her daughter [Justine], saying [that] she had not been raised to behave as she had done, she [Justine's mother], was very disappointed. (A letter from the West Virginia Department of Welfare, August 9, 1988)

In 1948, Justine Diehl left her immediate family behind, making her way to the Huntington area where she met and married Jack Ying (formally known as "Jack Ying Chan"). This relationship was a very unstable one, at best. According to my half-sister, Jackie, this was largely due to Jack Ying's mother, who never accepted the mixed marriage. This marriage produced two girls; Jackie and Mary Jean Chan were both eventually sent to live in a local children's home.

From varying accounts, at some point between 1949 and 1951, Justine Diehl Ying met, and began a relationship, with Julian Caldwell, a cab driver. During this three-year period, Justine gave birth to two boys: Stephen Anthony (1949) and James Curtis (1951). When the babies were born, Justine had the name of her then husband, Jack Ying, listed on the birth certificates as the father. According to the above-quoted report from the Welfare Department, Jack Ying stated that, under the terms of the divorce, Justine had been given custody of both boys. The question remains as to whether Jack Ying or Julian Caldwell was the father of Steve.

On February 20, 1951—approximately three and a half weeks after the birth of James—Justine approached Enid Tomblin, her usual babysitter, asking if she would take care of Jimmy. The sitter agreed. Approximately two months later, Stephen was placed in the care of the Tomblins. It was also between April and August 1951 that a divorce between Justine and Jack Ying occurred.

According to a conversation that Enid Tomblin had with the apparent sister-in-law of Julian Caldwell, Julian was the father of both boys. This account seems to be substantiated by the testimony of Jack Ying stating that "he was not the biological father of either of the boys, although they, [Jack and

Justine Ying], were still married and living together at the time
of their birth … and, therefore, was listed as their legal father."

All that being said, his testimony does conflict with his
daughter, Jackie Ying Sloan, who maintained that (according
to notes made during our phone conversation on November
13, 1992) it was clear that while we do have the same mother,
it is also apparent that we do *not* have the same father. She
remembered our mother bringing home a baby and letting her
hold the newborn on her lap when she was five years old. From
other evidence provided, it also appears that Jackie, Steve, and
Mary Jean were all the children of Jack and Justine Ying. Of
all the children in the Ying household, I was the only half-
brother—*not* being the son of Jack Ying.

Evidence discovered concerning the divorce revealed more
previously undisclosed information. According to Justine's
sister-in-law, there had been spousal abuse by Jack Ying, most
likely due to the mixed marriage, of which Jack Ying's mother
was vehemently opposed. Additionally, from all indications, it
was not Justine who filed for divorce from Jack Ying. Rather,
the divorce proceeding was filed by Jack Ying after Justine
"simply left," according to the account given by Justine's sister-
in-law.

Simply wanting to end the marriage—and thus the family
conflict—and under the terms of the divorce, Jack "gave Justine
their house [and] he took custody of the two girls, and she had
custody of the two boys." According to the attorney handling
that divorce, it was difficult to locate the divorce decree record
because the spelling of Justine's maiden name differed on
various records (e.g., Diehl, Deihl, Dheel, to name a few).
This also impeded my search for the truth. In September of
that same year, Justine sold the property gained in the divorce
settlement and remained in California.

Steve and I remained in the Tomblin home until July 1953. At that time, we were removed from that home and placed in foster care with the Lewis family of Milton, West Virginia. Mrs. Tomblin shared the events of the day we were removed from her home. Deeming the Tomblin home to be a less than healthy environment for us, the Department of Welfare decided to remove us, placing us in the guardianship of the State of West Virginia.

Mrs. Tomblin recounted a black sedan pulling into their driveway—and social workers forcibly removing us. She recalled Steve's last words as they carried him away, placing him in the car: "I'll be back for supper, Pappy!"

Mr. Tomblin tried to follow the black sedan to see where they were taking us, but the social workers were able to elude him by switching cars farther along the road. Saddened and heartbroken by the sudden loss of the boys, Mrs. Tomblin never saw or heard from the brothers again. However, she knew in her heart that one day she would once again see or hear from one or both. That was the reason for her overwhelming response to my calling her in 1992—thirty-nine years later.

The social workers had taken us to Milton, West Virginia, approximately forty miles away from the Tomblins. We were placed in the foster care of the Lewis family, and we remained there until our relocation to the DeJarnett home in Salt Rock, West Virginia, on January 11, 1956.

CHAPTER 15

THE CIRCLE IS COMPLETED

And that's the story.

Having come full circle to January 1956, the so-called lost years were finally recovered. "So what?" one might ask. Am I any better off knowing about those first four years with all the "drama" contained therein? Does that newly discovered understanding change those years that followed or my adult years since the discoveries made? I would have to answer, "No, not really." However, this fuller understanding has made me realize more clearly—and with a greater conviction of heart—that each one of us matters to the Lord. According to Jeremiah 1:5, He knows us intimately from before our conception in the womb and throughout our lives.

So, returning to my original question: Who am I? I am James C. Diehl, son of the late Julian Caldwell and Justine Olivia Diehl and foster son of the late Mr. and Mrs. Scott DeJarnett. However, more importantly than that, I am a son of my heavenly Father. He has carried me through all these years, growing and developing me to be an instrument in His hands. Oh, and the family I longed for, I now have one of my very own.

Some might read this account and express sympathy—or even feel sorry for two boys conceived in sin, abandoned by their earthly parents, and suffered through times of frustration and loneliness. Please do not do that. Why?

First, *everyone* has a story. It's called life, and each story is unique—even with some similarities along the way. What matters is what we do with that story. Do we wallow in the mire of self-pity or allow bitterness and anger to control our outlook on life? Absolutely not! We use those life experiences, allowing the Lord to grow us and prepare us to be used for His glory. We must always remember that, although earthly humankind will often fail us or even cast us aside, our heavenly Father *never* forsakes us—even when we fail and forsake Him.

This point takes me back to that phone call from Julian Caldwell in 1981. Having told me that he had let us down and "dropped the ball" as our father, I remember my immediate thought and reply to him: "Mr. Caldwell, yes, you did drop the ball as our earthly father, but I want you to understand that where you dropped that ball, my heavenly Father picked it up and carried us through all those years." Nothing could be truer or more glorious.

God's grace is not applicable merely toward our sinful nature from which He delivers all who place their trust in His Son, the Lord Jesus Christ. Absolutely not! Were it not for His sustaining grace at work throughout our lives—from conception on—we would certainly be left alone to grope our way through a life that often offers tragedies, misfortunes, and darkness.

I look back and say, "Thank you, Father, for picking me up when others cast me aside and let me fall, leaving me all alone in this world." Throughout these years, God, my heavenly Father, has provided for every need at the time I needed that provision. He has worked through many wonderful people—and even a very few not so wonderful persons—all of whom I have included in this account.

Lastly, it is truly amazing how the Lord takes all the circumstances of life and molds them into something truly marvelous. I began life as an abandoned little boy, having no permanent family, but God has blessed me with a wonderful family of my own. Over the years, we have been blessed again with our granddaughter, Bryleigh. What began as a story of abandonment became—and continues to be—a testimony of God's goodness and grace. What more could I ask? What more could I ever want?

Epilogue

Present Day

Throughout all of this, I am constantly amazed how the Lord reveals His plans for us. Several years ago, I had the distinct pleasure of serving on the board of directors of Davis-Stuart, Inc., having by that time directed its focus on "troubled" teenagers who had been involved in drug abuse or other situations that required them to be temporarily removed from the home. The average stay at Davis-Stuart for these teens was approximately six months—with the expectation of returning the teens to their families following counseling and rehabilitation for both teen and parent.

During my first term on the board, I attended a Christmas celebration meal during which the board members shared the evening with the teen residents. Upon learning that I had lived at Davis-Stuart as a teen, one of the residents engaged me in a short conversation.

"So, you used to live here?" he asked.

"Yes, I sure did … a very long time ago," I replied.

"How long did you have to stay here?"

"Five years," I said.

He immediately said, "Whoa—and I thought six months was a long time!"

I looked him directly in the eyes and said, "Son, those five years were some of the best years of my life. You can't understand that right now, but perhaps you will later."

In the years following my research for this story, I received additional information relating to my biological family and my extended family through the Welfare Department. First, Mrs. Ruth W. Manley stayed with the department for many years, becoming an executive of the department and overseeing the training of field workers. On one occasion, she invited me to be a guest panelist in a training session to share my experiences as a ward of the state and my thoughts on what social workers needed to better understand about their kids. I received a call from her daughter, Jane, in the 1990s, that Mrs. Manley had passed away.

During my research, I discovered two more siblings living in Columbus, Ohio. We share the same biological mother—but not father. Our mother, Justine, had left Julian Caldwell in California and remarried in Ohio. According to my newly discovered half-sister, Justine denied having any other children till the day she passed away. The only way this lady had found out about the rest of us siblings was due to some records that surfaced in the process of Justine's admittance into an assisted living complex. About two years after our initial contact, my half-sister called to inform me of our mother's death.

Both Mom Alcie and Poppy Scott DeJarnett passed away several years ago. I was both privileged and saddened to preach their funerals. I continue to remain in touch with Judy, and I have traveled to Milton, West Virginia, many times to visit with her and her husband, Perry. She is—and always will be—the best sister God could have given to me.

As for my brother, Steve, I have not seen him since 1971. We have been in contact via ham radio and phone calls over the years. He retired from the navy after serving for twenty-seven years. He has lived in Ingleside, Texas, since retiring. He has never married.

Karen and I have been married for forty-seven years and are still living in the Aiken, South Carolina, area. She works as a certified ministry assistant for the Solid Rock Baptist Church, and I am still the director of missions for the Aiken Baptist Association.

Both of our sons and our granddaughter live in North Carolina. Neither are married at this time, but we do have a terrific four-year old granddaughter. Bryleigh is now the child of a single parent, and the cycle continues. The big difference this time, however, is that this little gal has a loving family through her dad and through her "Nana K" and "PaPa Diehl."

What have I learned throughout all these years? More importantly, what do I desire for you to take away from this account? I have learned that God uses events and circumstances throughout our lives as a means of preparing us for whatever He desires to accomplish in and through us in the future. In other words, it's all a part of God's great plan for us. God gives us choices throughout our lives. We can either bemoan them and feel sorry for ourselves over the seemingly bad—or even tragic—circumstances this life affords or we can view those as being allowed by the Lord to prepare us for His work and then seek to glorify Him for the opportunity.

So, the story continues. I haven't a clue how it will end this side of heaven, but I do know this: His grace *is* sufficient!

Printed in the USA
CPSIA information can be obtained
at www.ICGtesting.com
LVHW091553300923
759618LV00040B/762